Lost and Found
and Other Essays

Lost and Found
and Other Essays

Rica Bolipata-Santos

The University of the Philippines Press
Diliman, Quezon City

THE UNIVERSITY OF THE PHILIPPINES PRESS
E. de los Santos St., UP Campus, Diliman, Quezon City 1101
Tel. Nos.: (02)925-3243, (02)926-6642 / Telefax No.: (02)928-2558
E-mail: press@up.edu.ph
Website: uppress.com.ph

First Printing 2010
Second Printing 2011

The National Library of the Philippines CIP Data

Recommended entry:

Santos, Rica Bolipata.
       Lost and found and other essays / Rica
Bolipata-Santos.—Quezon City: The University
of the Philippines Press, c2010. (2011 printing)
          p.;   cm.

          1. Santos, Rica Bolipata—Anecdotes.
2. Conduct of life—Anecdotes. 3. Life skills—
Anecdotes. 4. Self realization—Anecdotes.
I. Title.

BF637.C5 158.1 2011 P095000030
ISBN 978-971-542-634-3

Book Design by Zenaida N. Ebalan

Printed in the Philippines by Rightfield Printing & Supplies

Contents

Foreword

by Cristina Pantoja Hidalgo

She didn't think of herself as a writer. She was 33 years old when she decided to enroll in UP for a PhD in creative writing. But she had always been what she calls a closet writer.

The first class she found herself in was mine. This is her recollection of it.

"The story actually starts in Ateneo. My chair asked me what I wanted to do for my PhD. 'Creative Writing,' I said to her. And she looked at me quizzically, because no one really knew about my heart's desire to become a writer. So, on the first day of class in UP when you asked me what was my course, and I pronounced 'Creative Writing,' that was monumental for me. I was finally claiming it. The fact that you did not flinch or wonder or pause at my pronouncement was, I felt, a good omen."

Rica Bolipata-Santos is still short of her degree, but she produced one book which won the prestigious Madrigal-Gonzalez Best First Book Award administered by the UP Institute of Creative Writing; has picked up a *Free Press* award for the essay in English; writes a column in the *Philippine Star*; and now, here's the second book. This would give other writers, who have been at it much longer, some pause.

I recall receiving this agitated SMS message from her when the news leaked out that her first book had been chosen for the Madrigal-Gonzalez. "I've just been told that my book won a UP award. Is this true?" When I confirmed the news, adding that it wasn't just a "UP award" but a national one, she replied, "I can't believe it!"

The distinguished panel of judges—composed of J. Neil Garcia, Vince Groyon, and Jaime An Lim—cited her "luminous little personal narratives," for their "uncommon candor, grace, and humor," describing how she treaded "the uneven terrain of the quotidian with an open compass, unafraid to confront and scrutinize even her own intimate fears, insecurities and confusions," and emerging clear-eyed and convincing.

Love, Desire, Children, Etc. (Milflores Publishing, 2005) is now frequently taught in literature classes, and the warmth with which the author is greeted when invited to be a guest at these sessions is proof of how her thoughts and words resonate in her readers' hearts.

I was a member of the panel at the UP National Writers' Workshop (which is now for more advanced writers, not beginners) to which Rica was invited, so I knew this second book would be even better. I remember how amused I was when Rica announced, a little defensively, that contrary to what people might think from reading what she writes, she does do other things besides take care of her family and teach school. They're what she calls, with her tongue firmly planted in her cheek, of course, her "nation things," i.e., things she does for the larger community, for society.

"So why don't you write about those things too?" someone asked.

Rica replied that she tried, but that they never came out good enough to satisfy even her.

"Then perhaps you just have to learn how to write those better," someone said.

Rica agreed, quickly and humbly. She would try, she said.

But reading her *Lost and Found* now, I think to myself; this is contribution enough.

These essays are well thought out, carefully crafted, lovingly wrought pieces. But most important, they are deeply moving. Trying to put my finger on what makes them so touching, so poignant, several words present themselves—honesty, courage, careful attention to the nuances of emotion, to life itself.

Perhaps the author herself defines the quality, when she says in one of her essays: "To do this I must be truthful about my own self."

It is not an easy thing to do. And the book is replete with instances of the author's struggle to stand by that vow.

Confronted by a small daughter, wise beyond her years, who declares, "Mommy, I never want to be a mommy. I watch you all the time and it is just too hard," she whispers. "I fear the world for her."

Recalling her parents' marriage, she decides, "It was not a 'happy' one and I have come to the conclusion that to seek happiness in a marriage is pointless," but adds, "What stays with me and what I use in my own marriage is the idea of the necessity and nobility of sacrifice."

What comes through in the memory of her mother's prayer "Dear God, thank you for the talents of the boys and the goodness of the girls," and the many ways in which she and her sisters were expected to take a back seat to the brilliant Bolipata brothers, is her astonishment now that it was simply accepted as natural then. But recalling how those brothers—and everyone else in the clan—has come through for her time and again, she says, "I realize that as in all families, my family has given me a soft place on which to fall."

But for all that *Lost and Found* might be—in the author's own words—"an invitation to think about the things we hold dear and how we handle these things, and how we lose them, in spite of the attempt to keep them safe and sound," it is also a *fun* book. Because Rica is a fun girl, and a funny one.

Take her account of an encounter with the rich: "Wealth whispers its own set of rules and its rules are hidden somewhere between the three sets of spoons and forks I need to navigate. Never having been privy to them, I am at a loss." And her delightful memoir about the courtship that led to her marriage ("Sitting there in my flag-like blouse, I was floored, flummoxed, flabbergasted").

She is also an imaginative, think-outside-the-box, push-the-envelope kind of person. Reflecting on language, she says, "We use words differently and repetition is something that appears quite often:

pabaling-baling, pabandying-bandying, unat-unat. In Ilocano, very much is *unay-unay.* The repetition of words ... reminds me of being rocked. As if the word could do two things, describe and comfort."

The musical artist—the singer—in her hears the words like notes in her head. "When I think of the word 'hopeless', I think of this other beautiful word, despair. I think it is beautiful because it sounds the way it should feel like. The air at the end of the word seems incapable of flight because of the harshness of the consonants *d, s,* and *p.* This is what despair feels like—a yearning hampered."

But the collection is strongest when the author tells of the pain that would break many a heart, the constant challenge of bringing up a special child which grows more complex and more difficult every day. "I have learned how to be friends with darkness and confusion as I pause and wait ..."

Rica's talisman is faith. It is not just Catholic faith, the faith in a benevolent wise God, although there is that too. It is a faith in herself, in her capacity to endure, and her ability to find the right words, and to work them so that whatever it is that happens can be made sense of.

At the Baguio workshop, Rica was asked by another writing fellow—not challengingly, just curiously, I thought—what made her think that readers would care about the very personal things she writes about. She paused for a few seconds. And then she said, "I believe that the search for meaning is dignified."

And so it is. It is also beautiful.

August 2009

Preface

A good four years separate this new collection from the first one in 2005, *Love, Desire, Children, Etc.*, published by Milflores. Why so much time in between? Probably because I received what all writers crave and fear: attention.

Love, Desire, Children, Etc. begins with that honest line: "I call my writing a secret life." In fact for many years I called myself a "closet writer." Years later, I realize that I was in the closet a long time not because I was afraid (anyone with children eats fear for breakfast, every day), not because no one knew I could write and needed approval (are you kidding me?), not because I could not possibly have an audience (that is every writer's conceit: the belief that someone will always want to read me); but because to be in the closet meant a kind of unimaginable freedom—a freedom that does not take risks, that does not fear anything, that does not attempt to change anything. Perhaps a better word for the closet is "naïveté."

Well, that's all over and done with now. Writing a regular column for the *Philippine Star* since 2005, I had to leave an e-mail address where readers could get in touch with me. Through this device, I've received hate mail ranging from "You are certain to burn in hell" to "You have done nothing to improve the human race." In the beginning, my eyes would gloss over these painful words and I would wonder what about my very tiny thoughts could possibly upset someone from Albuquerque? After a while, and much rationalization, I was grateful that someone could be so angry enough to take the time out to write and tell me what they truly felt. There was power there too—power to make someone make a choice, as writing is all about choices. As I like to say in all my writing classes, "Writing is an act of identification." What you write delineates between what you are and what you are not.

At some point in the next few years, attending workshops, talks, meet-the-artist events, book launches, etc., I found myself having to answer the most difficult question of all: why should anyone care about what I write, if I write only about myself? Walking foggy Baguio, with the best and brightest writers of this generation, I was asked this question formally (meaning I had no choice but to finally give a good enough answer) and realized it is something many people want to ask of me. Who the hell are you and why should anyone care about your world?

My first response is a kind of reflection about the world of art and the way art conceals the artist who renders a version of the world. Each artist and artistic form uses a range of methods and strategies to do this and there seems to be a bias for artists who hide themselves more than reveal themselves, not knowing that masquerading and obscuring are strategies themselves in order to achieve revelation. At the end of the day, every piece of art is a metaphorical attempt of a human being to make sense of what s/he believes in, argues for, attempts to describe. In a sense, all art is personal; and therefore the question "why should I care about you?" is not only for the creative nonfictionist, it is a question for all artists. And yes, it is also a revelation of a kind of bias the consumer of art has, or at least does not know s/he has. My only question at the end of any interaction with art is to ask whether it was good, whether something new was revealed or something old was revealed anew.

There is absolutely no way I can answer this question completely and sufficiently enough for anyone. I can only tell you that I am aware of this question every time I attempt the innocent act of making my hands glide across a page. It informs my every working out of form, structure, and content. It makes me not want to waste anyone's time and it makes me honest beyond belief. I'm not sure if that's good or bad (I have already been placed in some circle of hell by some readers). I only know that some parts of me remain naive—the closet writer still inside me, I suppose. I truly believe that kindheartedness, or that old-fashioned idea of "good intentions," trumps *everything* in the end.

Lost and Found is a favorite theme of mine. The first collection closes with a fictional piece of the same title. Looking at the computer, I see that I have at least four unfinished pieces that bear the same title. I like the premise of such a dynamic. These pieces reveal that loss is a necessity and that being found is a promise because of the word "and" that joins them.

Lost and Found is an invitation to think about the things we hold dear and how we handle these things and how we lose them, in spite of the attempt to keep them safe and sound. The irony in life is how easy it is to lose that which we hold most dear. As if, as human beings we cannot help ourselves and ultimately want to see what might happen to us if we ... just let go.

What happens when one loses a parent? A friend? A best friend? A dream? Faith? Hope? Love? An old thought or an old self? A beloved belief? I sometimes wonder if we let go because it's easier: easier to surrender to the absurdity of loss rather than the strength of human will to keep at it, to keep living with consciousness, to find beauty in the Sisyphus in all of us. How hard do we fight the inevitability of loss and what does that say about us as human beings?

The pieces in this collection are a bit different from the ones in the first. These are all from my column and column writing has its own parameters. I am encouraged to not stray too far from the 2,000 word limit. Some of them exceed that and it is due to the kindness and wisdom of my editor that I am able to sneak in a few hundred more.

There is a kind of discipline in column writing that I enjoy. The readership is far more diverse and I have to keep myself concrete and specific. For some strange reason, the limited space allows me to "fly higher" with ideas because word choice becomes a real matter of life and death. Syntax means everything suddenly. And the discipline it takes every month to create or fashion a piece that will allow me to think about the heart of the matter, all matters, great and small.

My first thanks must go to *Philippine Star* and my editor Millet Martinez Mananquil who invited me to join the newspaper based on a eulogy I wrote. Whenever I submit something my heart always thinks it will never see the print of day, but Millet always surprises me, accommodates my ramblings on the page. There are the *Star* readers whom I must thank as well, especially those who have gone out of their way to write me, or correspond with me on a regular basis.

There are, as always, my first readers: Anna Galvez, Norman Agatep, Laine Laudico, Badong Abesamis, Manoling Francisco, Erwin Arandia, and Lou Grant. Of course, thanks as well to Cyan Abad-Jugo and Mark Escaler who keep folders of my works because they love me and have been dreaming with me for decades. There are the UP Writers Workshop friends and comrades who were there when I had to answer the most difficult questions in mid-career: Ian Casocot, Luis Katigbak, Allan Derain, Jun Lana, Jun Balde, Nick Pichay, Bob Añonuevo, Frank Cimatu, and Vincenz Serrano. My workshop roommates in Room 1 who have become women I run to in times of great doubt, Mookie Katigbak and Tara Sering. And the wonderful mentors and friends at UP: National Artists Rio Alma and Bienvenido Lumbera, Butch Dalisay, Gemino Abad, Jun Cruz Reyes, Vim Nadera, Charlson Ong, Joey Baquiran, Butch Guerrero, Marby Villaceran, and Ralph Galan; and most especially mentor and woman writer trailblazer Cristina Pantoja Hidalgo.

There are two other gods I must mention and give my thanks to: Greg Brillantes and Gilda Cordero Fernando. In what I believe to be a completely random act of generosity, Greg took it upon himself to find me, bring me 100 books and advise me on what to do next in my career. He sat in my dining room, as my children ran circles around him, remembering what it felt to have a wise old man in the room. He shared stories he had in the making and I threatened to steal one from him. Ha! He intoned that famous line: "You must finish your novel before you are 40." I raised my arms to include the kingdom of my domain, and asked "how?" He merely smiled. I suspect in true Greg fashion, that *that* was the best answer I was going to get. Since then, there have been coffee dates and funny phone calls and many, many hugs. When I feel particularly beaten by the act of writing, I have only to hold one of his many books and I am appeased in knowing I am not alone.

And there are those lovely moments with Gilda, who does not need to speak or do anything really to inspire me and countless others. But again and again, as I splay my heart all over her dining table, she picks up the pieces of my heart and calls them jewels. I am grateful for all writers who continue to father and mother me, whether I am conscious of them or not.

(And there is one other angel I must mention, Mr. Chito Tagaysay. He is not aware of how vital he was to my creative growth and knowing him he would rather remain unknowing so I will not say more. Except, thanks.)

And *of course,* to those whom I am mother, wife, sister, and daughter to—my boundless love and thanks. There is a plea for forgiveness somewhere in there, too. For certainly, there have been moments when I have been lost to them.

July 2009

Because You Asked Me

And so you asked me if I think you should start having children. I said to you "what?" I wasn't sure I had heard you correctly as my ass was creating a squeaking sound as it negotiated with a leather chair against my jeans, my left arm cradling my enormous bag I call the Mommy bag. These are my requirements for the perfect bag: waterproof, vomit-proof, big enough to carry a small thermos of water, or milk and two books, one for me and one for the baby. Someday my baggage will no longer be this big I tell myself everyday.

I looked at you more clearly, my eyes adjusting to a new height and proportion. Talking to tiny people all day can weaken the eye muscles. With a grown-up, they are razor-sharp again. I could tell you were disappointed at my not having responded yes quickly enough. But you see I couldn't.

I had just come from therapy with my son. Therapy with him sometimes blinds me. In that one hour, all that is wrong with him and all that is wrong with me comes to the fore and I find myself erased of hope. As I leave the therapy room after paying, a concrete act that can sometimes make me want to burst into tears, I am busy with the task of rebuilding again. I rebuild my son, myself, my family, the world, really. It takes immense concentration to be able to do this everyday.

But you are quiet, across from me because you know me well. You know it takes me a while to settle. You also know you deserve an answer. (It's scary because you're under the impression I know the answer.) I'm just hedging really. Inside, my mind is formulating an appropriate response. I want to be sure I don't dupe you with my answer. Like a well-trained teacher, I flip the question back to you. "So, should you start having children?"

"We were thinking about it," you tell me. "We're not getting any younger, we've been married quite long, there's enough money in the bank, we have secure jobs so it seems the right time. Plus, she thinks I'll make a great father."

That truly warmed my heart. It is a great compliment to be told you have promise as a parent. I looked at you. You were clear-eyed. Once again I realized people don't get it. You always have the answers. It's not the question that stumps. It's the answer because more often than not, the answer requires courage. That's harder sometimes. What did we have when I had my firstborn at twenty-seven? An apartment that ate up all our income, for one. But that's what I'm good at: mustering courage.

"So what are you afraid of? Let's list our fears and confront them. I'll be honest with you. What do you want to know?"

"Time. Will I still have time and sleep?"

"You won't have it anymore," I said outright. "You will have to learn how to catnap creatively. My mother-in-love tells me she still hasn't slept well since she took home her babies. You're just going to have to live with that. Next."

"Money. Will I have enough money?"

"No, you will never have enough money. Yes, you will lose most of your savings. But you will survive. Money isn't always about the baby—it's about the state of the world. You can't be a slave to money. Next!"

"Plans for myself. Will I ever be able to fulfill plans I had for myself?"

"I don't know. I've learned not to plan with children. I have learned greater skills though, like multi-tasking (putting kids to sleep and writing lesson plans in my head, for example). I also know how to write and read at the same time! It's cheating really but I've memorized my children's books so if pressed for time, I can "read" them the book while my hands type away. Can you imagine what processing my brain has to do! Next."

"Aren't kids so demanding?" I actually laughed out loud, almost near hysteria. I started to tear.

"Will I regret having a child?"

"Well, regret is regret. You could regret not having one as well. Regret is a good thing, I promise. I personally don't believe in not having regrets. I think it's misguided optimism. I believe more in the modernists. You have no choice but to choose! That traps you, but frees you as well. I embrace all that I've chosen and not chosen and am grateful for both!"

We were silent for a while. I think you were partly wondering if I'm crazy. I smiled, secretly relieved I am no longer asking this question. Glad that I have made my choice.

I am taken back to another conversation with a good friend who asked me the same question years ago before I became a mother. He was far more certain though about not wanting children.

"Why, Rica? Why have children? Give me one good unselfish reason. Don't we have children just for ourselves?"

I posed the question back to you and told you that three children later I still have no answer. I keep thinking if I knew the answer, I'd be better at parenting. You laughed and said wasn't it easy during the olden days when you HAD to have children for the specie to survive? One didn't have the time or the luxury to answer such questions. We laughed at that together. I remembered a grandmother in a loveless marriage bearing nine children until she bore a son to fulfill her husband's desire for immortality. On her deathbed, she refused to drink water her husband brought to her—a last sign of rebellion. I imagined what was in her head—"at least this last act is for me."

"But really Rica," you pushed further. "Why have children?"

I looked out the restaurant window and distracted you by ordering a sinful dessert—mangoes and cream. You didn't notice it but I became more flamboyant, more theatrical. I was doing this really so that you would forget the question. From where we were seated, I saw the car arrive and breathed relief. I should have told you that having children decreases social skills too. I shouldn't be let out of the house really.

I kissed you goodbye and you looked perplexed. You were hoping for some answer to that last question but I was not able to give it to you. On the way home I promised myself to give you a provisionary answer. So here, here now is what I would have said now that I've had time to let go of my Mommy bag:

Who understands the movement of the heart? One second you're reading a book, the next second a desire for a child comes into play. It's almost random, this wanting. Think of when you want something yourself. Doesn't it come at the most surprising times? It's just like a seed under all that fertile soil. What signals it to begin its ascent? Your heart is now fertile as well.

I am convinced that the desire comes when I am overwhelmed by love and it naturally spills (and yes, I mean that metaphorical pun of spilling sperm) over. Here, in bearing children, the crystallization of love complete. It begins with loving an equal. It becomes overpowering that the need to create becomes great. We all want to love, but imagine the kind of love you must learn to love your helpless, hapless creation. Human beings continue to have children, because they cannot help but love, just as they are burdened by having to choose. And we cannot love abstractly. Love must be concretized, incarnated. Yes, it is selfish, but wow! It is beautiful.

So there, an attempt at an answer, because you asked.

A Family in Faith

This is how we pray at night:

We pray one "Our Father," one "Hail Mary," and one "Glory Be." After which I ask everyone to say what was the best part of the day. I think this is my favorite part of our prayer—this choosing of what was best. They choose the most touching of things, and the most concrete items of life: seeing fish in their grandmother's pond, having warm *pan de sal* for breakfast, lolling around in bed with Daddy, reading books on the sofa with Mommy. After this part, we all then make a list of people to pray for. When they were smaller, this list was just as small— it contained only family members. Now that they are bigger other people have entered their prayer lists—friends in school, teachers, and other children they've met at the playground. And finally, our prayer ends when we recite "Angel of God" in unison. Right before the silence for sleep, I say "I love you" to them individually, just to make sure I get that across everyday.

I learned this process through my sister. This was how her husband's family prayed, she said. I wanted our families to know how to pray together so I used it as well. I thought that the act of choosing the best part and the people to pray for was a wonderful way to anchor the utility of prayer. Children learn best through concrete things and it feels like in praying this way, the path to holiness seems simple and clear: to pray means to set aside time; it means an examination of the day, it is learning to see Someone's loving hand in the way the day has been made, and it ultimately means gratefulness for all that we have.

This part of parenting, teaching faith and prayer and defining abstract things like faith, hope and love, has been a process that continually becomes more and more complex. I intentionally do not use the word "difficult" although it is an easier word. I prefer the word "complex" because it is more descriptive of how the process is something that does not ever become simple. The teaching, instructing, and embracing of faith is part and parcel of parenting for all time, I believe. Although they will someday have to grapple with their faith, on their own terms, their sense of values, their morality, the backbone of being, is ultimately taught through me and their father, and the example that we set (especially our actions and attitudes about faith) while they are young.

I have three children and they are in differing ages of belief. To teach them about Christmas, I've been reading to them this big book titled *Following A Star*, for around three years now. It is a simple book that chronicles the journey of Mary and Joseph to Bethlehem, the innkeeper's offering of a stable, and the different people who visit the Baby. When they were smaller, what attracted them most to the story were the pictures. The book is very big so the pictures are sumptuous to the eyes. They loved the animals! We would go through the different animals present at the stable and make their animal sounds.

As they got bigger, their interests began to change. They became interested in knowing the names of the characters. What were the Kings' names? What was the name of the angel? What is a stable? Why can't I tell them the name of the shepherds? It has become more and more challenging, especially since I am excited to give the whole story, to unfold salvation history, to underline concepts about my faith to them. But I cannot; for now the questions guide me carefully. I know they are signposts of what individually they are capable of understanding and digesting. Ironically enough, how I answer and what I answer is metaphorical as well, of me.

In one part of the book it says, "miracle of miracles did appear." My daughter turns to me and asks what a miracle is? I am stumped. I do not know how to explain concretely what a miracle is. She tells me that in school, she was taught that Christ's crucifixion is the saddest day in history. She says this matter-of-factly. My two-year-old tries to say the word "crucifixion." I know she's saying this to me because I need to explain it to her.

For a brief moment I am taken back in time and I wonder how I learned all this—the nitty-gritty of knowing what I truly believe in.

At the end of trick-or-treat, my firstborn reminds me it is time to take out the Christmas decorations. We put up the Christmas tree together as a family every year, while listening to Christmas carols and begin to make our Christmas lists. I learned this ritual from my own mother. As we did this two weeks ago, I thought to myself: am I doing this correctly? Surely I did not want them to think Christmas is just about presents? I watched them talk amongst themselves about what to ask from Santa and I was able to find inspiration from the book of Christmas. I asked them to tell me what the three Kings brought to Bethlehem. Their teeth got all mixed up trying to be the first to say "gold, frankincense, and myrrh." I told them that they too must find something they can bring to the stable. God gave us this child, what can we give back? They were frozen for a while and then my two-year-old suddenly screamed, "Hay!" The answer was perfect, for the moment.

Last month, we added to our repertoire of Christmas books. Our new book is titled *The Christmas Star*. It spins the story creatively. It talks about the different things that added to the light of the Christmas star. And so you have the wheat-colored hay that reflected the light. And you have the shiny back of the spider silently spinning his web. Even the bell around the cow's neck added to the shine of the Christmas morning. For now the new perspective of the same story enthralls them. Soon, maybe tonight, I will begin to talk about the difference between darkness and light. I will subtly begin to talk about how the birth of Christ pierced the darkness of humanity. I don't know how I'm going to do it, or what words to use so it will make sense, but I am excited to figure it out.

This was something I never knew would be true about being a parent: that in having children I would understand the saints. I look at these three borne of me and know what Mary and Joseph felt. I can understand the landscape of Joseph's fear when Christ was lost in the temple. I can feel Mary's anguish at Calvary. I wish I were more like them: Mary in her steadfastness and faith, Joseph in his strength and fortitude. I even understand why St. Augustine took so long falling in love with God. I know, with all my heart, why his mother, St. Monica, turned to Him for help. Because when faced with parenting, you instantly get it that you cannot do it alone.

These days, I talk to them about goodness and kindness and tell them about St. Therese's Little Way. Yes I tell them, goodness is in washing your hands before dinner. Believe in this! As my children put their hands in prayer position at mealtime and bedtime, I sense my faith become even more alive, even better understood and loved. How I wish this were a gift I could easily bestow on them. We bow our heads in prayer together, a family in faith. Through my children, I truly know what it means to have been gifted with light.

Nothing But the Truth

A few days ago, Marty, my six-year-old daughter caught me crying. She looked at me, her eyes wider than usual, and asked why. I'm not sure anymore what my answer was; I think something about feeling pain in my eyes because of the medication I was applying regularly. It was a lie of course, because the pain lay elsewhere although it did have something to do with an inability to see clearly.

I thought the eye excuse would do, but a minute later, she says to me. "Mommy, I never want to be a mommy. I watch you all the time and it is just too hard."

Marty's like that—she is astute and wise beyond her years—an indigo child if I ever met one. She sees right through me and understands more of the world than I did at six or even at twenty-six. She understands the simplicity of truth—of recognizing it and not being afraid of it.

When she was about four or five, she started to cry to me about love. "Mommy, when I meet my true love, do I have to marry him?" I asked her why, intrigued to find out where the fear was coming from. "Mommy, will I have to meet him? Does everyone have to have a true love? I don't mind having none. Will anyone force me to marry him?" I told her my own love story—my thrill in meeting her father; the relief in finding someone who loved me completely. Not to be assuaged, I told her to give herself some time and not to be so quick to make a judgment. That was surreal.

At moments like these, I find myself figuring out how to raise a daughter. With her, it is different. I fear the world for her. I am more compelled to protect her. I am under the assumption that the world has so many secrets I need to teach her. Perhaps because much of what is taught about womanhood is false or worse, kept secret. People who raised me never taught me about sexuality, femininity, true love, power, or grace. Faced with her honesty, I feel that I owe her nothing but the truth. And truth in parenting, sometimes, is very, very difficult to do.

To do this, I must be truthful about my own self. This process of truthfulness has encouraged me to reassess my understanding of wifehood, motherhood, and personhood. I try to balance all that I am, across all that I would wish to be, on a fulcrum of all that I must be, and the seesaw of my life balances precariously. How do I tell her at her core is a person? And like a child, this person is continually figuring things out. Motherhood does not make person perfect—only more aware of imperfection.

If she were to ask me if I am a good wife, can I say with full conviction that I am a good wife? This is my eleventh year of marriage and more now than ever, our differences have come to the fore. These differences could be lived with via a myriad of devices in the first decade—repression, suppression, displacement, grand gestures of love. In the next decade, I have a suspicion these methods will no longer work. How then to survive these glaring differences?

Marty sits on her father's lap during family dinner. She is having a hard time apologizing to a cousin she has hurt. I tell her that apologizing is necessary even when it is difficult. My husband looks at me and I wonder whom I am addressing. I look into Marty's eyes and tell her Mommy and Daddy say sorry to each other all the time. Her daddy silently mumbles, "Although Daddy apologizes more often." I am quick to retort, "Because Daddy is more often wrong." He corrects me, "No, because Mommy's pride is large." The gauntlet is thrown.

I look at the interior of marriage and wonder what it is I must say to Marty about true love and marrying your true love. When she looks at my marriage, what am I teaching her? How do I show her that happiness is work?

The intricacies of marriage rest on one simple ingredient: the capacity to sacrifice. Every day presents a certain kind of demand for sacrifice. Who showers first, what to buy at the grocery, who suffers leaving earlier with the banned car, who will bring the kids to the emergency room if necessary, who will put the kids to sleep because the other must study or work, who is in charge of ordering the birthday cake—the giraffe-shaped one, the precise kind the kid ordered because God knows getting the wrong cake spells the difference in all the world!

We make these sacrifices unknowingly, quickly, naturally even. They creep up on us as we think we are acting on instinct. What it has the capacity to do is to suddenly fashion a life that can sometimes be accidental. Did I really want to be here? I see my husband ask this question more and more these days. He has had to make the most sacrifices, it comes to me now; even if I count labor, afterbirth pains, and breastfeeding immeasurable and therefore unbeatable. Because of my choices to be a teacher, to quit work to rest my heart, to need time for reading and staring, to have time to sing and write, he has to stay put where he is, in order for me to ... daydream.

I have become good at this qualifying exercise—thinking marriage and love are things I can put in equations and make equal. Marty has begun to learn mathematical concepts and it looks very clear to her as they appear in apples and oranges. I tell her while we do her assignment:

"Marty, how many are Mommy and Daddy." She says we are two. I tell her, "What happened to Mommy and Daddy when they become two? Do we dissolve into the number two and disappear?" She looks at me quizzically because she knows me well. She knows it's a trick question.

The other week, she began to have tantrums practically every day. Eventually battered by having to deal with tantrums from my special son and my daughter and my toddler, I collapsed in tears and told her my heart could not take it anymore. I begged her to release me by just telling me what it was that bothered her so. Her answer was simple: "I want to be special too, Mommy. I want to be allowed to have tantrums."

I was rendered speechless by such honesty. She has begun to resent it actively that her own assertion of self is compromised by the presence of siblings. She is younger than her brother, but because he is special, she must give in to him often. She is still a child, but because I rely on her to help me with the toddler, it is demanded of her to be of service. These are things I never felt the need to question. But she is absolutely right. Her tantrum is an act of defiance. And yet she must learn that no matter how much she might want to be alone, she will always be shape-shifting herself because of the presence of someone else. That's what it means to be family, I guess. Or what it means to be human.

We play this game Lemonade when we wait in the car for her brother to finish with therapy. It is one of the few ways to get her out of a bad mood. She resents having to wait for a brother who will probably pinch her when he gets in the car. In the game, we sing a song that determines what part of us will disappear. If the song ends with you clapping last, you lose first your hand, then your arm, then your shoulder, until you are rendered armless. In play-form it is funny. We look at the new shapes we have taken and laugh even harder when our arms reappear. In love, and life, it is not always so funny. What wise child thought of such a game?

We teach our children relentlessly and hope that what we teach will be enough to help them find their way. Marty will soon tread the world of the painful grade school years where peer pressure lights the way. I must be a beacon of truth. I must remember that to do that, I must always be truthful to myself, like she is.

Later on, she revealed to me what it was that scared her so about finding her true love. The answer was very simple. She said, "Mommy, because it means I will have to grow up." She is absolutely right.

Lost and Found

It should not have mattered to me, and yet it did. Reading the news that Angelina Jolie and Brad Pitt are expecting a child caused such overwhelming sadness that caught me by surprise. What was it that truly saddened me?

Partly, I must have been depressed by the fact that a large part of my reality is decided upon by media. In magazines and television shows, I partake of this Western culture. I see it in the way I am embroiled in Brangelina (a made-up name for Brad and Angelina's affair). How, oh how did Jennifer Aniston suddenly have a place in my life?

Reading the news online, my mind began to wander and imagine. I could see Jen (yes, I imagine we are close) in her Malibu home, her chiseled abs showing through her yoga outfit. Her perfect, famous hair must have been slightly messy, what with all the tossing and turning she had to do the night before. I presume she's been tossing and turning since October, when her divorce was finalized. She sits there waiting for the bomb. Media has been rife with rumors about this pregnancy. Everyone is waiting. She's hoping Brad will tell her himself. Instead, in my imagination, she finds out from her manager, who calls her.

I tried to invent how hearing the news might have felt to her. What words would she have used to define this event? Would she have called it a betrayal? Would she have called it tragic? Who knows, perhaps she would have called it …? What words would she have used to describe her feeling? Anger. Sadness. Regret?

With confirmation of all that she might have suspected, what must alter ever so monumentally is this weight of memory she has of

Brad. Instinctively, she will have to go back to the past and figure out where the chain began to rust. It all looked so promising, she would think to herself. We think the same thing as we recall all the perfect pictures we've seen of them in various red carpet events. She is always in the perfect dress, he in the perfect suit. They gaze lovingly into each other's eyes. It looks as if their joy is real.

She will revisit conversations. She will try to figure out what promises were made. She will try to guess if she looked desperate or strong near the end. Naturally, all the memories move back and forth and she will be confused as to what was true and what was merely imagined. For sure she will attempt to answer the question, when was love lost?

For such is the case with any loss, whether trivial or serious. We plunge into our memories hoping to find the definitive moment when something fell through the cracks, as if zeroing in on a specific moment (yes, that moment during dinner when Jen admitted she didn't like Brad's taste in furniture) can help in dealing with the loss.

Here, in my own life, as Jen struggled with losing love, I was struggling with having lost my purse. I was in Makati waiting for a meeting and decided to wait at a corner coffee shop. I had two bags with me: a black purse and a forest green briefcase. My meeting was a good two hours away, and as usual, I decided to while the time away writing. My black purse was on the chair to my right and the green bag on the chair to my left. The tables beside me were empty. I must have written only a good ten minutes when I realized that my purse was gone.

The purse and its contents were dear to me. The purse itself I had bought on a free trip to Bangkok my husband and I took two years ago. I had just delivered my third and last child and it was our first trip alone, together, since we had started on this journey called parenting. In the purse was a small make-up bag my sister had given me from her trip to Belgium. All three of us sisters had this same make-up purse in different colors. My journal was in it as well—a Moleskine journal given by Butch Dalisay himself. Moleskine journals were what Picasso

14

and Hemingway used as their everyday notebooks. Mine contained first lines of essays I was planning to write. They contained text messages from friends and family that I did not want to lose. They contained comments from writing workshops I had attended. Even more painfully, I had placed a picture in between its pages—a picture of me at six, singing onstage. The discovery that all that had gone, in the blink of an eye, was painful. I could not even remember how much money I had in it. It did not matter to me at the time.

Like my imagined Jen, I find myself in the coffee shop repeatedly. I think if only I had placed my purse on my lap instead of on the chair. I see it in my head and know that I was easy prey. If I had left my previous meeting later maybe someone else would have been the victim. When was the purse taken away? It is a pretty big purse and how could it have slipped my eye. I do the same replay game as Jen. We, Jen and I (yes, we are almost like sisters now), replay to check the veracity of what we remember. We replay (I see Jen nodding, agreeing with me), because we want to understand why what happened, happened. We go through the steps, second-guess choices we've made and try to make sense of the ambiguity and absurdity of it all. We replay to give ourselves the opportunity to be wiser, better or faster.

A few months earlier, in May, I lost my father. I look back to April when he went swimming with my children. I look back to February when I gave him a new alarm system so he could call his nurse more easily. I look back to January at the beginning of the New Year. I replay to torture myself and wonder if I would have acted the same if I knew he would be gone in a few months time.

At night, I think of what I would say to Brad. This is really what I want to ask him: do you mourn losing Jen? Because this is what upsets us, we who have to speculate on celebrity couples breaking up. We get upset with the pace with which people move from lost to found. We are upset about how easily celebrities move from love to love. We (this time I am in sync with the readers of the tabloids) think that loss should be honored. We do not think spending time in the zoo with Angelina is honorable at all. We want loss to be recognized. We want it to be given its proper space.

15

To Jen, to me, to anyone who has lost anything dear: what do I imagine I would like to say to you?

I always think of this paperclip I had lost as a kid. I loved this yellow paperclip for some strange reason—maybe it was the shape I loved or the color. One day, I lost it. I remember clearly understanding for the first time loss: that it could happen so easily, no matter how vigilant one was, no matter how much one loved something, or someone.

A few days later, I found it among my clothes. Such joy at the revelation that it was only lost to me. Because that is one thing Jen and I can take hope in: things are never lost completely. They are put away. They are misplaced. Someone else takes them. Sometimes, they are transformed into something else. But nothing ever disintegrates or disappears. That precious paperclip lies somewhere in this world—it must have a new shape, or a new color, or even a new form. Just like the love you have for someone who has gone. That love does not disintegrate either. One day when you least expect it (this I can imagine because I am a romantic), you will find that things are less ... achy. You will be amazed at how much the heart can bear. And yes, you and I will be grateful for all that we've lost and all that we've found. In time.

On Romance,
True Love, and Marriage

Dedicated to Gilda Cordero Fernando

Almost twenty years ago, on a regular school day, someone came up to me and asked if he could set a meeting with me. I looked at him, this unusually tall man, and wondered what it was he could possibly want to say to me, an unusually short girl. We were in college then, and once, a year ago, prior to this, when I first saw this man, my heart did a little jump and I heard it whisper, you will marry this man.

Although I was prone to flights of wisdom, I was also prone to flights of fancy, which made it easy to be critical of my inner voice. Surely the inner voice whispering such a certainty was a product of the imagination. This man, as he stood there waiting for a reply, I could tell was ... nervous. He had a look of unease although he did his best to hide it. Maybe it was his nervousness that made me say yes, and so our meeting was set for February 10 and we agreed to meet by the college library at 4 p.m.

I arrived around 4:20 because I had almost forgotten about our meeting. I was wearing a red, white, and blue blouse with jeans. He was there already, with a backpack on, and we climbed a few steps before we settled on one. He started to speak and truthfully I wasn't listening very well as the view was fantastic. I was swinging my legs when I began to *really* listen. He said,

"I've been watching you and I have this compelling need to know you. It's gotten to the point where I get upset at how other people

17

know you so well. I don't know what this is—if it is love. I just know I had to tell you."

Like all stories, he has his own version of this event. I love the way he finds me in his version. His side of the story includes watching me from afar as I walked from class to class for many months. It includes a nervous bus ride with his best friend the night before he asks to see me. His version even includes a moment of enlightenment while eating a value meal at Wendy's.

But there is something I love more to this story, no matter whose version is on the table. At the moment of this meeting, all I know is this man saying such unbelievable lines. He knows so much more though. He knows me in a way I don't know myself. He has brought new elements into my life: the idea of being watched, the notion of being compelling to watch and therefore beautiful, the knowledge he has shared of other people knowing me well, the possibility of love. Is this not romance? The ingredients of a great love story are in place. There is recognition ("You will marry this man"), there is desire ("I have a compelling need"), and there is conflict ("I don't know what this is").

Sitting there in my flag-like blouse, I was floored, flummoxed, flabbergasted. Four days later, I had my first official, real Valentine. I was excited to see what he would present to me. It was not at all what I had expected: clumsily, he placed six oranges in my arms. It was certainly a taste of things to come. It felt heavy in my arms, and quite strange. How un-thematic, I thought to myself. How ... healthy.

On our first Christmas together, I surprised him with a fully decorated Christmas tree, set in the corner of our tiny apartment. Our trimmings came from our first trip abroad to Germany and I myself had painstakingly arranged the lights around the tree. But this wasn't the best part. The best part was presenting him with a brand new camera—a grand romantic gesture to signify his role as chronicler of our forever!

On Christmas Eve, he surprised me with his own present. There were two pieces wrapped in newspaper. I opened the present and found four ill-shaped knobs. I had no idea what they were for. He said to me, "They are for hanging hand towels in the Guest bathroom," which of course, did not exist in the apartment. He took out another present. I tore through the newspaper and saw it was a rod. "This," he said, with pride, "is for hanging bath towels." The disappointment stuck in my throat like bitter medicine. This was not what our first Christmas should look like, I thought to myself! Why was he giving me household items for presents? Alas, there was still another present. I opened it and in it was a piece of wood with four wheels. He said "It's a lazy Susan so that it's easy to pass food at the table." I couldn't help it but I started to cry. And finally, he brought out one last piece and it was bigger than me. I opened it and found a large mirror. And my romantic moment finally came. All these different pieces—the knobs, the rod, the lazy Susan, when put together formed a full-length mirror. "This way, you can see yourself every morning." It was a sweet gift because our apartment had no mirrors. The present seemed a continuing metaphor of the idea of his enjoyment of watching me.

These of course all happened more than a decade ago and such romantic moments no longer happen to us, or happen rarely. Time has whittled away our capacity to be romantic. Because that is the central problem that tugs at the heart of true love and romance. True love demands knowledge of someone intimately. It requires constancy and commitment. The heart of its mystery lies in a person's ability to know you so well that the person chooses to still love you, in spite your ugliness. Romance, can sometimes look like it lies on the other side of the spectrum. Romance works with a different kind of mystery—with the desire to know someone that can be inexplicable. It begs for attention, which explains the grandness of its gestures: fleeting gestures that have great impact for the senses, but not always for the soul. True love is a product of time. Romance, on the other hand, hinges on newness, novelty, and surprise. In the romantic mind, you wish to sleep with someone and look beautiful in sleep. In real life, you snore and drool in sleep, but—and it's a big but—there's no one else you'd rather sleep with.

I have come to a greater understanding of this major difference now, now that we are older. For a while, it was difficult for me as I naturally crave romance, live for romance, need romance, especially in sustaining my creative life. What does one do if one has discovered the "pearl of great price" which is love but constantly needs romance? I've discovered the most important secret of all: the greatest romance is the one I have with myself. It might sound crazy, but it has helped me sustain a balance.

Yes, I romance myself. This means I continually try to see myself anew. And so, I cultivate my inner life. I go out with myself often. I pursue friendships that enrich me. I go on adventures on my own. I surround my space with beauty. I do not wait for presents, surprises, nor bows or ribbons from another. I put the energy of expectation onto myself and make myself responsible for my happiness. That first mirror from years ago, which still stands in our bathroom, is a reminder of this gift he has given me: the capacity to see myself everyday.

I find romance in the activity of retelling our story, especially to our children. I find romance in nostalgia, in memories, in holding mementoes from the past like love letters and pressed flowers. I no longer equate romance with love. After all, this is a guy who played the violin for me, sings Jose Mari Chan songs when I can't sleep, stayed with me in the delivery room, holds my hand in any waiting room, covers me with a blanket every 2 a.m., buys me a journal from every port he has been to—he no longer needs to prove love. He is exempted from all my romantic expectations. For without expectations, I become capable of being truly surprised. Because finding true love, and being found worthy of love, is the best surprise of all.

We just passed February 10, our first, authentic anniversary. I look at my husband and wonder, especially on endless days, if he sees that girl he was once so compelled to look at. And always, always, just when I get to a point of enormous doubt and I get ready to summon the maturity to accept I'm old and romance is overrated, he does something to keep the romance going, in his own special way.

Just yesterday, while I was reading, he sat beside me, opened an orange and fed me. He looked at me and we grinned at each other, transported to that funny valentine when he placed six oranges in my hands. What could be more romantic than shared history? My, how healthy love can be.

Why Travel?

I arrived in Virginia eight hours ago after a grueling 24 hour trip. First there was the flight to Narita that took three hours. And then there was a layover in Narita that lasted a good four hours. And then the almost unbearable-any-moment-now-I'm-gonna-scream eleven hours from Narita to Chicago. By this time, a tiny cold I had been nursing in Manila broke out in full force making landing terribly difficult for me as the change in pressure would make my ears hurt. Our group would spend almost five hours in Chicago waiting for our connecting flight to Virginia, where we arrived near midnight. Two of my oldest friends, Erwin and Hector, who have made Virginia their home, came to collect me and we stayed up until 2 a.m. playing catch-up. Exhausted, I took a nasal decongestant and fell into a dreamless sleep. I did not even have the strength to call home.

Pico Iyer once famously asked, why travel? Well, that's easy enough to answer. I traveled this far, and left my children, to go with Bukas Palad on a six-city tour to sing for Filipino communities abroad. For twenty-five days, we will be singing in almost ten concerts! We are scheduled to sing in New Jersey, New York, L.A., San Diego, and San Jose. We've been preparing for this tour (the group's fifth in its twenty-year history) since February and my days and nights have been kept busy learning new songs and, gasp, learning new dance moves. At the end of every concert we sing the old Hotdogs songs "Manila" and "Bongga Ka Day!" So why I am here? is pretty easy enough to answer.

But *why* am I really here? Well, that will take much more honesty.

Why Travel?

I am not a traveler, by nature. I do not look at pictures of faraway places and think to myself, "Someday I'd like to see that place!" I do not read books and wish that I could live in distant lands. What I want to live out in books is experience, not place. Naïve of me to think of course, that experience and place are two separate things.

Strangely still, physical landscapes do not move me as much as I think they should, no matter how beautiful they are. Fortunately, I married a real traveler. My husband likes to move a lot and since we've been married, we've been to some interesting places. I'm certain that without his prodding I would never have moved! But he is a force on his own so once in a while I will be cajoled into leaving and seeing a new place. We've gotten into an easy rhythm when we travel together. The first two days, I indulge him and walk the ends of the new world with him. (I remember on our honeymoon in Hong Kong how exasperated I was with his need to ride all modes of transportation available!) By the third or fourth day, when I feel I've earned enough brownie points and convinced him I'm REALLY an adventurer, I beg for my quiet time and ask to be left alone. He continues on his adventures, and I continue mine in my solitary world. Our friendship is strong enough for this.

A couple of months ago, my husband and I found ourselves in Greece. Walking around Athens, I realized a major difference between this land and my land, something I would never have realized if I had not left home. Their history is part of their present. Ruins abound and city dwellers are reminded again and again of their ancient great roots. That must make a major difference in the modern Greek psyche—to always be reminded of what one had accomplished. Not the same back home. History is not where I live; history is in some faraway place like Manila or Malate or Intramuros. I know, this is partly my fault, of course.

We stayed in Athens briefly for we had decided to visit the smaller islands rather than visit the more cosmopolitan cities. Standing by the seaside of Oia, I asked myself if I had seen anything more beautiful. Why yes, I thought to myself. It looks exactly like Zambales. Nestled between the Zambales mountains are a group of islands in Pundaquit. It takes forty-five minutes by boat to get there, but it is a breathtaking experience and one that always moves me to tears. How strange to have traveled so many miles and see with my own eyes how special my land is. So yes, Greece was beautiful and different and maybe I'd go again. But when I think of magical places in my imagination, I do not see Oia.

Months before the trip, friends who have been kind enough to take me in, e-mailed regularly to ask what it is I would like to see and do or what retail outlets I would like to visit. Oh my goodness, I honestly replied, give me a tiny spot of stillness and I will be happy. For neither do I travel so that I may accumulate more things. I already accumulated so much more than necessary, in preparation for the trip! For this travel, I had to buy boots, sneakers, a plethora of jackets, and even new underwear ...

It's a funny experience, preparing for travel. You buy many different things so that one, you may not be so surprised with what you might find far away from home. You anticipate the difference in weather and so the necessary clothing that comes with such an expectation. You are sure your handy dandy medicine for colds and cough will not be available there, so you bring a *banig*, or two, or three. You are certain things will be more expensive abroad, so you make sure to buy everything you might possibly and logically need so that you do not waste your dollars. My handbag is a testament to this not wanting to be surprised by the foreign. I have Decolgen, Kremil-S, Advil, Bonamine, Alaxan, Salonpas gel, and my ever reliable Bohrer-Ding, a Chinese mentholated stick that works wonders for headaches and body aches.

But more strangely, you prepare for travel so that you may duplicate the experience of being home, while far away from home. To duplicate the experience of home, I brought with me books—a sure way to make me feel comfortable anywhere. My old slippers are with me, together with my comfiest pajamas. I have brought pictures of my children and my keychain has a picture of my husband in it. My sister is far more extreme. When she travels she even brings her own sheets! Hotel beds or friends' beds are turned over and blanketed in familiar sheets that smell of home and hearth.

It is perhaps this resulting duality that makes traveling more than anything, an attempt at self-identification. In traveling, you find yourself perpetually in the land of in-between. You are, foremost, a foreigner. A couple of days in a new place, the foreign-ness will disappear and you will get comfortable enough once you see that human beings are the same wherever they are. But by the time this happens, it is time to leave, because no matter what, you are still foreign. You set up a version of a home no matter where you go, but the large suitcase by the bed is a constant reminder that you are merely passing through. You will make friends and promise to e-mail, text, and write. But once the distance has been set, not all promises will be kept. The weight of luggage is a constant reminder that your final destination lies elsewhere.

In the "Land of In-Between" is where it is possible to find one's self. In travel, you are allowed a split personality. Without the bearings of home, you are left to figure out who you are. Without the trappings of the familiar, you are able to defamiliarize yourself. Because no matter whom you leave behind, and no matter whom you might bump into when you travel, you will never be able to escape yourself. For the next twenty-five days, I am allowed to cast-off parts of me I will not need to play. I am not mother, daughter, sister, teacher, or wife. Without the familiar routine of these roles, the adventure begins. And maybe that's why I eventually stop resisting the invitation to travel: because I can never resist traveling to myself.

In May, I will accompany my husband to Istanbul. I am told it is a breathtaking place and is always on the list of places to see before one dies. I wonder who I'll find there.

A Room of One's Own

Would it be awful for me to say "I want my own room?" Nothing thrills me more than articulating ideas and feelings that are often thought, but rarely spoken. Many of these thoughts are unspoken because we are frightened to say them out loud in fear that we will be judged selfish, unnatural, and immature. But surely I am not the first married woman to think such a thing! Was it not in 1929 when Virginia Woolf beautifully said, "A woman must have money and a room of her own if she is going to write." Of course, you could take away "if she is going to write," and change it to any other passion a woman may have. Credit a forward-thinking woman to think such a rebellious thought! Of course, credit must go to her forward thinking husband too.

One of the hardest things to navigate in marriage is the carving out of space, and I mean private space or personal space. Perhaps because we presume that love is the enlargement of many of our spaces—the spaces between bodies broken by sex and children; spaces between hearts broken by vows of eternity; spaces between lives broken by intimacy. And even the space between yours and mine, broken by the shared bank account. The romance of marriage lulls us into the belief that we are one and that all sacred spaces are shared from this moment forward.

It was something I certainly bought into the first few years I was married. Did I ever want to eradicate spaces between my husband and me! How I wanted to absorb myself into him and he into me! I'd like to think he felt the same way, in the beginning as well. We did everything together! When we built our home, we made our room big enough to incorporate all the different spaces of our lives. And so our room is a bedroom, a TV room, a workroom, and even a playroom.

But, it has been more than ten years now and the gloves have come off. My husband has finally come to the conclusion that I am messy and that I come with too much clutter. I tend to agree.

As a teacher, my life is built around books and paper. On any given day, I am certain to come home with papers from students. I read an average of five books a week, often all at the same time. This is just my stuff as a teacher. There's stuff too as a writer. Now there are even more books and paper strewn all over the place. And just to make things clear, he's not uncluttered at all. There's his stuff too: a thousand and one receipts he claims he needs but never quite brings to work. There are his man-things, golf balls, print-outs of advice on how to become a better golfer, earplugs and blinders he insists on keeping, a variety of calling cards he claims he needs to keep but months later can no longer remember who these people on the cards are.

And of course, the children have absolutely no sense of space because as far as they are concerned, everything is *their* space. They flit in and out of rooms as if our house had no room divisions. You can literally follow the crumbs on the floor to find where they have finally deposited themselves. More often than not, they would have deposited themselves on my bed.

Every day, the first hour of my new day is spent re-erecting divisions of all our lives. I file the same papers, put away books into respective shelves, return toys from under my bed (how I wish they were my own toys ...), go through a variety of things, deciding the fate of inanimate objects' lives, classifying all into *his, mine, theirs, ours.*

And so I say to my husband and my children, "May I please have my own room?" They do not understand what I mean. We are at an impasse because it is easy to take personally the need to stake out my own space. How easy the need for my own room to be labeled a rejection of the people who love me most! But it is simply not true.

Perhaps a need for my own room is a simple need to reclaim my own personal, sacred space.

As women, we are educated to share spaces. We are taught to be giving, accommodating, and compassionate, not because we are human beings, but because we are women and it is what we do best. We are taught to be unselfish, caring, maternal, nurturing, not because no one else can do it, but because it is presumed no one else has the *natural* instinct to do it.

And so it becomes *first* nature to us to give of ourselves in all things. Having been taught that to share one's life with a husband is the goal of all womanhood, we celebrate having reached this step. And then it becomes expected for us to bear children, for it is the height of what can be achieved by a marriage and we give literally everything to do this—our bodies, our time, our ability to invest in other things such as a career. As women, we do this automatically, sometimes without question. But always, somehow, at some point, whether we deny it or not, when we think to ourselves, well what about me?

The other night I went to dinner with another couple who spoke about their children. They were sharing with my husband and me their current decisions about their family and they always framed their decisions with the words, "*Para sa mga bata.*" They kept telling us about how much they were willing to sacrifice, including their own dreams and aspirations for their children. I knew they wanted me to nod vigorously, but I could not.

You see, I don't understand it. I don't think I was put on earth to save my children. I don't think I would be a good parent if I sacrificed myself for them. If anything, I think it teaches them to be afraid of the future. I think that if I were unhappy, they would know and they would wonder. And because children feel everything but cannot articulate the complexity of feeling, I am scared they will think they are the cause of my unhappiness. If we think that our children deserve to be happy, why does my happiness mean any less?

I want my children to watch me claim my own dreams so that they become brave to claim theirs. I want them to see me pursue my own dreams so that I never pass on and expect them to fulfill mine. I want my children to realize that their mother is a person and is entitled to the same chances given to them. Our children define words by how we live them as their parents. They need to see "bliss," "fulfillment," and "true love" personified so that they can achieve it too.

This unusual belief costs a lot. It might make me seem unnatural and selfish to others. It erects a space where others have no access to me because for me to fulfill my dreams might mean to put myself, as an individual, first sometimes. This space I so long for, this room of my own, is a physical manifestation of that individuality—of saying, this is mine and mine alone. But it is this inaccessible space, ironically enough, the allowance of this solitude, that allows the other spaces to enlarge, to welcome others for me to love wholeheartedly.

Confessions of a
Romance Novel Addict

L et me tell you a secret. Promise you won't think ill of me? Promise
me you'll try to understand? Promise me you'll still respect me in
the morning?

Okay here it goes: I'm a romance novel addict! Aargh! I can
almost hear the collective grunt of despair! Have I not spent a fair
amount of my time on the page talking about Literature with a capital
L? Have I not, again and again, admonished *Star* readers to make sure
they take the time out to read great books for great knowledge?

Well, yes. Reading romance novels certainly does not negate that
advice nor cancel out that belief. I'd like to think, and I guess you
could call this belief denial as well, that being able to read romance
novels allows me a more balanced view of reading in general.

But wait, what do I mean when I say I'm a romance novel addict?
Simple. Much like a druggie (of course we all have our own choice of
drugs, not necessarily the chemical kind), I read around four of these
novels in a week, so that comes out to around sixteen romance novels
a month. So yes, around once a week, normally around Wednesday or
Thursday, I will find the time to run away, sneak off into the mall,
enter a bookstore, and buy five or six titles. I think I normally buy in
the middle of the week, because I find it easier to survive the rest of
the demands of the week with these books by my side.

I have become methodical in choosing. It doesn't take me more
than twenty minutes to accomplish the task. Sometimes, I choose by

author. After almost two decades of reading romances, I am quite adept at this. There are authors from my childhood, for I had first learned of these novels from my oldest sister. These authors are Essie Summers (one of the safest authors I've read! Her characters sometimes don't even kiss until the last page of the book!), Margaret Pargeter, Yvonne Whittal, Janet Dailey, Mary Wibberley are authors I enjoy because their women characters are strong-willed, opinionated, savvy; although more often than not, they are still secretaries or assistants to their love interest. Sometimes, I choose by title. I myself love thinking of titles so I like to choose books using this criterion. Very seldom do I choose by plot, primarily because a love story is a basic plot.

Through the years, I've seen the changes in themes and situations in these novels. Before college, the power between men and women was always askew. Men were rich, powerful, and dynamic. The women were often underlings, inferior in rank and in stature. After college, the playing field became more level. The rise of the powerful female came to the fore and you now had women who had jobs, who were successful in the world. The landscape of battle happened now in the boardroom, as well. And as for sex, well, in the old novels, this rarely happened and women often saved themselves for marriage.

These days, a new kind of heroine has appeared on the pages. It isn't rare to find a woman now who has been divorced, widowed, or even pregnant. Women characters now are more forward, often engaging first in the sexual game. Women characters can act now like men. Which means, in the beginning of the novel, they are often obsessed with work, have no time for love and are jaded and cynical about love. The romance novel indeed has undergone many, many changes. And for some strange reason, I do feel wiser and better for having witnessed it in my reading.

I think romance novels have shaped a lot of my personality, and I mean that in a good way! I think in the beginning, these novels helped me have a good idea of what I would want love to be. Reading the power play between men and women in these pages, I knew I did not want to be in a relationship where a man would be stronger than me;

or God forbid, if he were stronger, to wield that strength over me. I also learned a lot about reading the signs men put out to show women that they are desired.

Nothing beats curling up with a romance novel on a rainy day! It's a great way to decompress the tired brain from all the work it has to do! After all, part of the appeal of the romance novel is the element of fantasy. With less than two hundred pages, characters often recognize instantaneously their attraction or a sense of belongingness or wholeness. Readers will enjoy that fantasy the most! We all want to believe that the One who comes to us comes to us naturally. We all want to believe that love descends like a thunderbolt, strikes us dumb, and we are never the same again. (And thank God for that!)

As a teacher and as a writer, romance novels continue to appeal to me because seriously, nothing is as difficult as writing a love story! The novels I read are not more than 180 pages and it is always amazing to me how an author is able to make closure within those prescribed pages. I am thrilled by the choices of obstacles an author can select from. Make the man a business magnate, have half his face deformed from a fire, make him a widower with a young son, make him cold-hearted and bitter because of the betrayal of his first love, make him a fugitive from a foreign land and then have him meet a woman who is a waitress, a hired woman for dating services, a secretary, a divorced mother of two, a runaway with amnesia, a wife already in a marriage of convenience, a princess in disguise!

For the love story to fly the author must make their love authentic. The author must call upon different methods to make sure that the transformation (for that is ultimately the point of all love stories-to document change wrought upon by love) of both characters is something readers can buy. At the end of 180 pages, the man and the woman must remain mere mortals who find in the other, a way by which their mortality is transcended. Because that's another reason why romance novels last—they make the idea of mortality bearable because it is faced with a loved one. And of course, all romance novels are built on a premise—that true love will prevail, NO MATTER

WHAT. It is the ultimate fantasy. You enter the novel filled with obstacles but we all know that those obstacles will fall away and love will triumph in the end! What better psychological medicine can one find?

As I write this, I am reading "The Wolf's Surrender." It is cheesy to the point of illegal satisfaction. The man is a judge and the woman is a lawyer. She has just delivered another man's baby in his chambers good Lord! I anticipate the author's machinations of character and predict already in my head how all these obstacles will be slain. How ridiculous! How silly! How impossible! Oh how fun!

Difficult People

L ately, I've been thinking about difficult people.

You know who I'm talking about, right? There's the difficult person at work, for example, maybe a boss or a team member. That's the person who lives to just make your life unbearable. I mean, the very idea of having to see this person in the office makes your daily routine for getting ready take longer than usual. She's the person who makes you sigh in resignation about the unfairness of life just as you punch in your time card. He's the one who makes you drag your feet into the office. She's the one who makes you check out the classifieds every weekend for a possible new job. Let's face it. At work, there are a myriad of ways to make life miserable! Maybe he does it by being discouraging or negative about all of the work you do; by making you feel your work is never good enough. Maybe he spreads gossip about you or tries to convince everyone you're not to be trusted. Or maybe she does it by making the simplest of things, say like, getting staple wire for your stapler, a tiny form of a power struggle. I swear, sometimes, work can feel like a version of high school politics all over again.

There's the difficult person at any given time while you're doing your errands. Maybe it's the person at the bank who doesn't know how to get in line. Or maybe it's the cashier at the grocery who bangs the stuff you bought as she punches them in. This is my pet peeve, actually. I've written many letters to large groceries to tell them to make their employees more polite and friendly. Or how about the person at the grocery who insists he should go first because he has fewer items? It can be the person at the bookstore who doesn't really know what you're talking about when you're looking for a book, looks at you uncomprehendingly, then passes you to another saleslady. Or it's the unbelievably verbose person at the end of the line, when all you want to do is order a cheese pizza, but she has been trained to offer you everything on the menu, all the specials, and all the new deals you can avail of. "Please! I always say, just a large cheese pizza!"

There's the difficult person on television or government (wait, why am I putting these people in the same category automatically?). Like the person saying the news who always gets the words wrong. Or the newscaster who looks like she's about to go to a party right after the telecast what with the green eyeshadow. There's the politician who doesn't know what he's talking about and doesn't mind telling everyone how much he doesn't know by the volume of his voice. There are the old politicians whose loyalties I can no longer tell because of their constant shifting from year to year. There are the annoying government officials who proclaim to all and sundry that all is well, when everyone knows with every fiber of their being, that all is NOT well.

And then there are the difficult people you live with. These people are harder to escape and take so much more work because you want to love the people you live with, but sometimes their presence is just unbearable. There's the husband who just can't do anything right. He's messy, he's ape-like, he's insensitive, he's never truly present "in the moment" and never romantic enough. There's the toddler you just can't please no matter how much you try to do so. Toddlers are infamous for having crying fits over existential things. For example, your biting into a cookie before giving it to a toddler makes him cry. Books say it's because he thinks he's the cookie. Go figure! There are the housemates you live with who destroy brand new clothes, break things because they're not careful enough, or spend the afternoons talking about you in the neighborhood. Sometimes they are the hardest to live with because of all that gray matter that stands in the way between you two—class, money, education, the rolled dice of life that doesn't make sense.

Every day I wake up it has become harder to deal with difficult people. I've been wondering if this inability to deal with difficulty is a function of age. The older I get, the more unbearable the battles seem and the more I dread going out of the house! These are the days I want to stay in and just read and have coffee and be left alone in my world. But the needs of daily life impinge upon me, knock on my door, and won't be left unnoticed. At any one point in any given day, I must face the difficult co-worker, the difficult cashier, the difficult husband, the difficult child. In all our imaginary worlds, we collectively imagine living in a place with no difficulty. We create the most encouraging officemates. We imagine running our daily lives with ease and speed. We invent the perfect world at home—fashion the perfect world to look like a spread worthy of appearing on Oprah's magazine. Sigh, sadly, this is not to be. The creases and wrinkles of life dog our existence.

I once read a poem (which unfortunately I can no longer remember) that thanked difficult people. The poem's premise is that difficult people make it easier for us to define ourselves. Difficult people help us assess what things matter to us; which form the core of our being. The difficult people at work shade more clearly for me what is important work and what are merely distractions. After all, why stay if it is truly difficult? Choosing to deal with the difficulties of a job (or a marriage, or a friendship) tells me what matters most to me, what causes are worth fighting for.

Difficult people show me my own capacity to be patient and kind. Yes, the person who wants to get ahead of me in line is annoying, but it won't hurt me to make him go ahead, right? Yes, it will take some time, but I can help the saleslady understand the categories of the bookstore so she can serve other customers better. Yes, I only want a cheese pizza but maybe I can listen anyway to what else is available. Maybe it is time to try the pepperoni. And yes, I can be a better wife and mother—by taking the time out to understand my loved ones' own difficulties.

Difficult people clearly show me that I have standards—in service, in what I expect of people, in what I would like my country to be. Difficult people show my impatience with dishonesty, with politicking, with selfish interests. Difficult people show me what traits I never want to have. No way will I be uncheerful, negative, hard to live with, inconsiderate, impatient, immature. No way will I be a gossipmonger, destructive, dishonest, or not forthright. No way will I be like you, or you, or you.

And maybe most importantly, I relish the realization that these decisions of who I am, and what I can be and what I will never be, make it difficult for other people to be with me. I like that. I like the idea that I can make things difficult for other people, as well.

Life Longing for Itself

In our house, my parents kept a mounted copy of the poem of Khalil Gibran titled "On Children." As a child, I would read the poem whenever I would see it. In the beginning, it seemed like good practice for my reading. After a while, I guess it was more habitual. I'd enter the room and my eyes would naturally move to the poem and I would read.

I have come across the poem again—almost accidentally (of course, there are no accidents ...) and it struck me in a completely different way. The past few weeks this line from the poem has haunted my thoughts: *Your children are not your children*. I have been reciting this, almost like a mantra. I finally understand it now.

In the beginning of parenting, it is easy to believe in the romance that your child is simply an extension of yourself. After all, everything about the process that makes them come into being seems to proclaim that truth. They would not have been born without your, um, full cooperation, so to speak. Ideally, they are born from an outpouring of love between two people. As a mother carrying a child in one's womb, you lull yourself with the idea that you are co-creator in the kingdom of God and your ability to create life puts you on some higher level.

And lo and behold, when a child is finally born, you recognize instantly your child's face as yours. That's still one of the most amazing things about giving birth—how your child looks just like you, acts just like you, sounds just like you—a mini-me, as a matter of fact. Society helps us believe that. When a baby is born, we are quick to decide who it looks like the most at once. As if it were impossible for a child, to look only like himself or herself alone. After all, what could be more appealing than the idea of rebirth?

Oh but as in all appealing things, this should come attached with its own warning sign of danger because at some time, at some point, a child will begin to assert his/her independence. I'm not really sure who has a harder time figuring this out: the child who must figuratively eliminate his/her parents to fully claim his/her own identity; or the parents who must come to terms with the fact that their children are not children anymore.

I have begun to feel this struggle now that my children are getting older. In the beginning, I made sense of their world through my eyes and figured it looked exactly the way it did in mine, after all, I rationalized, "we are so alike!" And so I built categories for them based on my personality. (I assure you, I did this all unintentionally!) Yes, my oldest son, like me, likes music and theater. And yes, my daughter, so like me, likes reading and quiet. Oh and my other boy, so unlike me, more like his father, into basketball and golf. I've used them to make their existence something about myself—a mirror image, a likeness, a foil to my own self. And even worse, I've used them to make me look good in my eyes and in the eyes of the public.

I get it. *My children are not my children.* I will admit it now, much to my dismay, my children like the songs of Willie Revillame.

But there's something far more mysterious and rich to think about. It is another line from the poem—"*They [the children], are the Sons and Daughters of Life's longing for itself.*"

I love the idea of Life desiring something for itself. It is an idea that moves me. To believe that Life has a natural progression and that it seeks to complete that progression in the continuation of humankind. These children who are born are born for the world and Life to complete itself.

Why then, are there children who are different? Or who are special? Or who are wounded? Or who cannot be like other children? I have one such child and it is his presence that makes that line from the poem confusing to me. If we are to accept the premise of the poem, how could the existence of this child help in Life's fulfillment? *What do we have to learn from special children in this life?*

I think that special children allow us to be more kind to each other. One's patience and love are tested when dealing with children and so much more with difficult children. I struggle with this every day, at the moment when I anticipate my son's tantrums or his violent outbursts. I try to make sense of it when I do a catalogue of all my wounds, and his as well. How patient was I? How loving was I? I always thought my goal was to make him a better person. Ironically, he has made me a better person—by extending my human kindness, by the constant chances he gives me to muster even more love. This happens in public too when people watch us. More often than not, people are kind to my son and to us.

I see this even more with his brother and his sister who have to make sense of him and how his life changes their lives. I am always amazed at how my younger children, have fashioned themselves to make room for their older brother in their lives. Once, after a particularly painful episode, my daughter came crying to me and said, "I can't believe how much I love *Kuya*. I could actually feel his pain."

I think special children allow us to see if our society is doing enough for all children. It is easy to gauge how far we have come as a society in terms of what kind of education and protection we give for all children. But then, what do we have in place for other kinds of children? What measures have we put in place to make sure they can become productive in society? What have we promulgated to make sure they are cared for? How much attention have we given special children? Do we look upon them with love, or with fear?

I think that special children help us to see that it does take a village to make a family. We have a tendency to isolate ourselves from each other, when things go well. But the dynamics of a family with a special child changes all that. Special families would not survive without support systems from their extended families, from schools, from communities and hopefully, someday, from government. The presence of these children forces us to think of others apart from ourselves.

These children show us different ways of being family. Our household is so large. We have doctors and therapists and teachers who come in and out of our house. My son is everyone's son in this world.

And maybe special children help us to filter what is truly important in life. I'm going to be honest and tell you that when I think of my life and my assessment of it, my only gauge is how good I am as a mother. It is this category that means the most to me. No matter how much I have accomplished in my life, and no matter how much I will have accomplished in the years to come, I never truly feel successful unless I have done my best as a mother, every day. Yes, I am hard on myself—but it's a gift my children, and most especially my special child have given me: a healthy sense of who I am and what my real purpose is: it is almost impossible for me to lose my way. I am the bow and my children are the arrows. My eyes are set on the future and its promise.

> *You are the bows from which your children as living arrows are sent forth.*
>
> *The archer sees the mark upon the path of the Infinite, and He bends you with His might that His arrows may go swift and far.*
>
> *Let your bending in the archer's hand be for gladness;*
>
> *For even as He loves the arrow that flies, so He loves also the bow that is stable.*

On Marriage

I have had three guiding voices in the keeping of my marriage.

The first comes from my theology class with Fr. Dacanay while in college. He impressed upon us students that the union of marriage would not be possible without the grace of God, sanctified in a union witnessed by the community. And that is why we marry in ritual and in public at that. As a man and woman, we call upon God, Christ, and the Holy Spirit to bless our union. We do this in front of a community because we call upon them for support as well. It is very clear to me that a marriage, although is worked on by two people, involves a bigger and greater community. Which is also why when other marriages are in trouble, I feel it is my responsibility to come in and help as well, in any way I can.

But what has made Fr. Dacanay's class even more real to me is the understanding that my humanness and my limited human love would not be enough to hold together a marriage and a family. There is no way I could remain married unless a greater force than my love for my husband is at play. Because certainly the longer one is married, the more marriage becomes brittle, dry, and desperate. Without the grace of God, I would not be able to make this situation a moment where greater love and understanding and patience could be born.

The second voice comes from Fr. Francis Reilly who had witnessed the growth of our love and officiated at our wedding. When we first came to him, he, in his usual quiet but very firm way admonished us to "prepare for your marriage and not for your wedding."

That was my guiding light as we were thrust upon the preparations for a wedding in the province with almost 400 guests! The admonition was so strong that a week before the wedding, I left all the preparations to my sisters and went ahead to the province to be quiet. That one week before the wedding itself allowed me to pray. The time to pray made it possible for me to be more aware of grace. Without the worries of the details of the wedding, I spent all day reading and writing, preparing myself to be a Bride. And so I approached the wedding day, not just with much joy, but more so with great peace.

At the wedding ceremony, we chose the Wedding of Cana as our Gospel reading. Fr. Reilly's sermon focused on what we should do to make sure our marriage remained strong. He used Mother Mary's own words. He said, "If you are not sure of what it is you should be doing, simply do whatever he tells you to do."

That has kept my marriage on course these past twelve years. With the coming of children, and the different challenges that come with a growing family, I have often found myself lost and afraid. More often than not, I am clueless on how to proceed with most things! I am constantly plagued by questions regarding the children, my career, my life path, and struggles with friends and family. But I am reminded again and again of Fr. Reilly's reminder to me. "Do whatever He tells you to do." I utter it like a mantra, like a spell that will certainly break the darkness.

To be able to know what He wants me to do is to be aware that God is active in my life. To mean that and know and live that actively myself takes great faith. It takes even greater faith to be able to discern what it is He actually wants me to do. It presupposes an existing language between me and my God. I have learned to trust in this relationship and in the language we have built together in prayer. I have learned how to be friends with darkness and confusion as I pause and wait. It is not always easy.

And my last guiding voice has been my parents' own marriage. It was not a "happy one" and I have come to the conclusion that to seek happiness in a marriage is pointless. I could say many things about my parents and like all children I could give a running critique on what was wrong with their marriage. But what stays with me and what I use in my own marriage is the idea of the necessity and nobility of sacrifice. A central ingredient to a marriage is the ability to sacrifice. One cannot be egocentric in a family. I saw my parents' different kinds of sacrifices and I am aware that to be able to sacrifice stems from an ability to truly love selflessly.

We are bombarded constantly with the message that our happiness is most important and that it is the goal of all things. Sacrifice has become a bad word! But I see now that life has to be more complicated and that it cannot just be about the pursuit of happiness. I think maybe it is more a pursuit of how to be more like Christ (and you can substitute this word with Enlightened or Fulfilled). And to want to do that or be like that is a Cross-filled path. The premise of a marriage is instantly about being with others in the world. Husbands and wives and children make compromises every single day to accommodate the actualization of each one. (Just think of what families have to juggle what with work, school, soccer practice, ballet practice, school performances, etc.) It takes tremendous love and support to do this for each other and yes, it is painful.

Last January, my husband and I celebrated our twelveth wedding anniversary. We left the children with my parents to have time to just be together. We made many lists on that trip. First, we made a list of the things we like about each other. Our lists surprised me. He liked my positive outlook in life. He liked the way I took care of the children. I liked the way he made decisions—the way he led our family life. We both had the quality "smart" on what we liked about the other.

Then we made a list of things we would never be able to change about each other—things we would need to already accept about each other. The list was revealing too primarily because it illustrated best how different we truly are from each other. There is his love for rooms being dark versus my need for rooms to be filled with light. There is his constant need to be in action while I thrive on the constant need to be still. I think he never looks at anything long enough, while he thinks

I take forever to look at everything. He eats fast, I eat slowly. He likes to travel and I am basically happy where I am. His adventures are physical, while mine are mental. He is extremely private while I have a very public life. He won't eat *lengua* (which I love) and I won't eat sushi (which he loves)!

There we were, under the moonlight in what we had hoped would be a romantic getaway and instead we had come to the conclusion that we had very little in common now that we are older. He turned to me and said, "Let's make a list of what we have in common then."

We agreed that we loved our families and that raising our family is a major priority. We agreed that we both love the sea and that it's okay that he uses it for swimming and I use it for meditation. We agreed that we both wanted to help our country, me in my writing and teaching and he in his own work. We both agreed that we both love God and that we would strive harder to make Him part of our lives. We ended with a list of our personal goals and our family goals.

What this story simply illustrates is an idea of what to project for in the future if you are thinking of getting married. When you look at the list of what we like about each other now, it is not what we started with when we were young. If you had asked me twelve years ago what I liked about him, I'm not sure these would be the same qualities! The second list speaks of a marriage that is strong and solid because the list reveals 1) how much we know about each other and 2) how much acceptance there is for each other. I think that's key to living together successfully. We have gone beyond trying to change each other to a healthy and even humorous understanding of each other. Our love is strong enough to accommodate these differences. There is nothing more romantic I think than knowing that someone gets you, knows you and holds you so well that there is no need for pretending.

At the end of our getaway, we prepared to come home and the familiarity of a life together kept me warm and safe. The easy rhythm of packing bags, of who brings what, who checks drawers in the room one last time is a balm to a crazy world where inconstancy prevails.

We stopped by the grocery on the way home and accomplished our list in thirty minutes. I asked him why we were rushing and I must say my heart was gladdened when he said he wanted to be home for the children. We ended the day with a Mass with them and I prayed that God bless our union once more. I looked at him three chairs separate from me (as the children took those seats). I remembered walking down the aisle and how I burst into tears seeing him waiting for me at the foot of the altar. We walked together up two steps to face our presiding priest. His very first words to Fr. Reilly were, "isn't she so beautiful?" I felt his beauty in this remembrance. I understand more now the mystery of sacrament—of how this mundane, regular life is so much more. It is because it has been taken, raised and offered and He in turns transforms that and makes it sacramental, blessed. And that in turns make greater love possible and faith real.

Long Time, No See

Next weekend is my father's first death anniversary. We're celebrating in a big way and consider this an official invitation to the public! On May 27, there will be a memorial concert for him at Casa San Miguel in San Antonio, Zambales. It is a whole afternoon activity for friends and family that begins with a tree-planting at 3 p.m. and culminates at 6 p.m. with a concert featuring the Pundaquit Virtuosi, Myra Beltran, Paul Morales, sons, daughters, and grandchildren. My brothers will be playing, my sister will unveil a mosaic she has been working on for months, and I get to read a poem.

I can't believe it has been a year since he left us. His death actually, was what brought me to *Philippine Star*. Doris Magsaysay-Ho, a cousin of mine, was at the wake when I delivered his eulogy. To honor my father, she asked me to give a copy of it to her. A few weeks later it appeared in the *Star*. My mother always reminds me that this space on the page, was my father's final gift to me.

I have been dreaming of him often. In the beginning, my dreams of him were long and looked like short, short stories. In short, they were dreams with plot and characters. These days, the dreams portray him in everyday scenes. I can imagine my psyche spinning out these tiny images—Pa on the computer, Pa in the garden, Pa turning on the lights, Pa walking to his room. I'm not certain why the theme of the dreams have changed. I am only glad that the dreams continue. For me, it is a sure sign that he is still in conversation with me. I can imagine him saying, "See, I've watered the garden here!"

My father and I always communicated well. He was always very clear about what he wanted me to be and what he wanted for me. As his last child, he had finished with the rigmarole of expectations with his older children. With me, he had realized that his role as a parent was to make sure he gave me as many options as possible. Perhaps with discipline and guidance I would be able to choose well. In a way, I fulfilled many of the dreams he could not fulfill because of his own constraints. More than anything, my father wanted to be an engineer and a writer. As a working student and scholar at the Ateneo though, he could not afford the equipment necessary for Engineering. The Law was the next best thing and it encouraged him to make use of his love of words. Perhaps that was why he allowed (and supported) all his children to fulfill their dreams. Disappointment and compromises were too familiar and I guess he wanted to shield us from that.

When I was six, he called me into his large office. This office was considered sacred ground and we were not allowed to play here. He did a big song and dance about setting a meeting with me. He sat on his large chair, and I sat with my feet dangling barely able to peer above the desk piled high with papers. Our topic for this conference, he said to me, in all seriousness, "was about your not eating breakfast."

He began to lecture me about the digestive system, taking the time out to draw a figure that represented my stomach. He told me about the acids that churned inside of me. Rubbing his hands together, he said, "those acids need something to digest. If there's nothing to digest, like these hands that rub against each other that have nothing in between them, friction will result, causing heat and causing pain. Someday, those acids will be strong enough to eat your entire tummy." I'm sure that by this time my eyes were large and frightened, and I promised to never skip breakfast again. He shook my hand and brought me to the door. That was far more effective than being scolded and berated I must say. Spoken to like an adult, I had no choice but to act like one.

My father's special gift was the ability to execute "grand gestures." He was not an emotional man, so he spoke no flowery words and did not know how to be comforting or consoling. But if one needed a knight in shining armor, a companion at war, a rescuer, no one could do this better than my father. Almost as if he couldn't help himself, he would effortlessly rescue family members, provide help, both financially and emotionally. For a while, his children, emotionally hungry for his kindness, found it strange how he could afford to be kind to others, more than to us.

I think what I hunger for more than anything is to see him. He used to say to me whenever I'd visit as a young wife, "long time, no see." I always knew it was part *lambing*, but also part admonition. He did not like it if people did not go out of their way to see him. Even if I was married, and a mother, the imperative to say hello was always part of my practice. Arriving from work, from school, from travel abroad, first thing on the list was always to peep into his room and say hello. Today, I cannot travel abroad without passing by his plot at Loyola Memorial.

It is the smallest of things that remain with me—the smoothest hands for example. Even as teenagers, my sisters and I would ask him to wash our hands. The neat toes and toenails, I would sometimes cut myself when he did not have the time to go to the barbershop. The faint stubble on his chin, salt and pepper in color, which I used to take out using tweezers! Yes indeed, long time, no see.

But the dreams keep me tied to him. Every morning when I wake up remembering his presence in my sleep, I am comforted no end. I'd like to think, these are not just dreams my psyche have come up with to console me in my grief. I'd like to believe that he appears in my dreams, because our love is so strong.

In the Beginning Was the Word

Gosh those Europeans really got it right, didn't they? They had the perfect word for the feeling one gets when there are no longer any words for what one feels. They called that angst—a German word in origin. In the enunciation of the word, you get the feeling of it as well. The way those last three letters bump into each other are perfect in describing bumps in real life leaving things off-kilter. Sometimes the bumps are so major that life (or the parts of life) just never become ever right.

But there's a French word for more or less the same feeling—ennui. Pronounced as an-u-wee, its magic is in the lengthening of the vowels that produce the effect of things taking longer than usual. Sometimes like sorrow or sadness, they linger and leave an imprint of grayness and it takes tremendous effort for life to get back some color.

The dictionary on my computer gives the formal, strict definition of both words. It says, "ennui is a feeling of listlessness and dissatisfaction arising from a lack of occupation or excitement." Angst on the other hand "is a feeling of deep anxiety or dread, typically an unfocused one about the human condition or the state of the world in general." This might be macabre, but the definitions seem comedic to me. Both definitions bear the stamp of seriousness and yet both recognize that what they attempt to do is describe feelings. And what could be more impossible than finding words for how we really, truly, madly, deeply feel?

But other things make me chuckle existentially because of the other words that surround the definitions. Listlessness reminds me of people who have run out of things to put on lists which might explain the latter half of the definition—of having nothing to occupy oneself with. And how about the unfocused anxiety about the condition of the world? Is this word a feeling or a state of being?

There are other words that I find interesting because of the way they look, the way they sound, and the way they combine a variety of other words to come up with new words for difficult situations. Here's another one: disease. Take it apart and it really is dis-ease—an inability to get into the natural ease of things. It makes one wonder why we get diseases. Maybe because metaphysically disease begins with a recognition that the body is in dis-array?

Really we owe much to the prefixes "un," "dis," and "in." When used in combination with other root words, they point to a world that we wouldn't want to live in. Dis-satisfied. Dis-content. Un-appreciated. Un-imaginable. In-equality. In-justice. The oppositions created help map a territory of what should not be in-cluded in the good life. What would we do if there were no words to help us demarcate the regions of happiness and un-happiness?

I look to the Filipino language and am enthralled with our own words that cut even more deeply into the heart of things. Such as this word—*agam-agam*. It could be the sister of angst as it also speaks of a fear and an anxiety. You know that feeling, right? It sits like a rock lodged somewhere between the heart and the throat and it becomes difficult to swallow. Sometimes the agam-agam is un-called for but something tells you your prediction might be right. To me, it speaks of the Filipino (and this of course refers to me) and the ability to read the signs of trouble way ahead of time.

We use words differently and repetition is something that appears quite often: *pabaling-baling, pabandying-bandying, pabalik-balik, unat-unat.* In Ilokano, very much is *unay-unay.* The repetition of words remind me of being rocked. (And here I will have to be honest and say I am not a linguist, but only a practitioner of words and my experience with them is the same with the experience of music. My understanding is intuitive and childlike, not at all informed by theory.) There is the sensation of going back and forth in the word. As if the word could do two things, describe and comfort. As if our ancestors knew, once was just not enough. (Or maybe because deep down, we're just silly. And I mean that in the best possible way.)

Or how about that feeling when one has a fever, lying in bed, trying to find the perfect position to achieve comfort when in dis-ease. That word is *pabaling-baling*. The body twists and turns and attempts to find its place, maybe not so much in order to flee the disease but maybe because of the need to know how to live with it. Pabaling-baling is a picturesque word that makes one see the bent knees, the shifting ass, the curled hands underneath cheek. "Finding the right position" just doesn't quite capture it all.

Filipino words are like top of the line cameras with incredible zoom features. They click on the context and attempt to render the entirety of it all in one word. *Kapatid*—not just brother or sister, but someone whose link I share with. *Bahaghari*—not just rainbow, but a king so mighty that his undergarments moved across the skies and filled it with color. *Nagdadalang-tao*—not just pregnant, but actively carrying (not even a child) but a full human being. *Maykapal*—not just God, but a dimension.

Ay Naku, we say. *Susmaryosep*, we counter. *Anak ng pating*, we exclaim. And in the '70s it was the "*patuka na lang ako sa ahas!*" an expression I've always' wished would return. And the ubiquitous "*ano*" that stands for anything and everything! It is noun, verb, adjective, direct object, symbol, metaphor, joke, the mish-mash of an entire world in a word.

O ano?, she said.

Pupunta lang ako sa ano, he said.

Anong bibilhin mo, she added.

Ano lang, yun lang, he explained.

And all was understood.

I sit here in my tiny room and try to find the perfect word for what sits in my heart. Ennui definitely. Angst always. *Ngunit, puno ng pag-asa, nanatili, nananahimik, nauudyok mag-isip ng mabuti, at higit sa lahat, malalim ang tiwala sa kinabukasan.*

Please, no translations needed. My reader knows what I mean.

Why I Did a Vagina Monologue

Well, you could say because I was born for the theater. Oh how I wish! But really, my earliest childhood games were about setting up plays with my brothers and sisters. Most of our days were spent (especially endless summer days!) under the direction of Jed, the eldest. He took charge of script, music, and rehearsals. Chin and Coke were in charge of set design and we girls were in charge of tickets and posters. This is all in my memory of course and maybe we all did everything together! We called ourselves The Young Players Group and ... we took ourselves very seriously, as children are wont to do when playing.

And so, when Missy Maramara, the theater actress asked me ever so casually if I wanted to be part of a school production of *Vagina Monologues*, I barely resisted! The call to play was just too good to pass up. In case you've been living in a cave the past few years, the *Vagina Monologues* by Eve Ensler is a series of monologues based on interviews of all kinds of women about their vaginas. These monologues discuss a variety of women's concerns: menstruation, intercourse, childbirth, rape, sexuality, etc. Its tone is honest and forthright.

I did the play partly also to—how do I say it?—authenticate myself as a teacher and as a member of the academic community. Five years ago, the school tried to put up this play and it was met with amazing opposition. The school was literally polarized—members who were utterly against staging it and members who were just as fervent about the validity of staging it. There was debate, forums, and endless discussions, a true testament to the power of the content of the play. At the end of the day, it was not staged.

Five years ago, I did not know where I stood. Certainly, in my heart, as an artist, I felt very much oppressed by the idea that another artist was being censored. But there was a teacher in me too, and a mother—a niggling, nagging feeling that my students might not be mature enough, or prepared enough for blinding enlightenment, yet.

To find a way around this, and to maybe grapple with the issue a bit better, I took to teaching the play to my students. Play as text is a different thing altogether and surely enough, as words, meaning is easy to grasp. A text is linear and logical and one only has to unravel written words on a page. Staging a text is altogether a different story. On stage, light, music, tone, costume, set are added and a text becomes fluid and multi-dimensional. I wanted to provide that for my students— and so as a final class project, we decided to stage, not the vagina monologues, but our own monologues, and so men had to give their own penis monologues as well.

And there we were, all seventeen of us, including myself and we delivered these monologues and because they were in an artistic form, they were insightful, tender, truthful, and extremely powerful. Really, it is true, that the truth will set you free. This experience made it easier for me to understand concretely the two sides of the coin, so to speak. Now I was certain which side I was on.

The monologue I was given was entitled "Hair," and it spoke of a married woman's experience of her husband asking her to repeatedly shave her hair "down there." We were pretty much left on our own to figure out interpretation and I read the script repeatedly and read this character as someone who had survived a traumatic experience, but who had managed to escape and so therefore was saying this monologue in order to tell other women, that one can leave such a situation. To me, the monologue was a testimonial to a woman's strength of character; it spoke of a woman's choice of one's Self over the desires of another.

After delivering the monologue the first night, I was told by some of the other actresses (we were around twenty composed of teachers and students), that I was not angry enough or pissed off enough. That jarred me and made me think of my interpretation of this character. Was my reading of her inner peace more a reading of myself? I looked at the words once again and tried very hard to muster the anger. (I suppose anger on stage is far more interesting to see than reconciliation.) And I did find the anger—against her husband who made her do something she did not like; the anger in dealing with the pain of shaving one's hair; her anger against the therapist who blamed her for the husband's infidelity. But I played the anger only up to that point. In the end, I tried (tried being the operative word here) to play her as a heroine. These are my character's last lines: *I realized then that hair is there for a reason. It's the leaf around the flower. It's the lawn around the house. You have to love hair in order to love a vagina. You can't just pick the parts you want. And besides, my husband never stopped screwing around.*

And I guess I did a Vagina Monologue because I wanted to push myself and feel the exhilarating power of terror! As a woman almost in her 40s, I have felt the imperative need to push my own self, especially against what people (what we call society—that mass of strange people we blame everything on) think I can do or should do. I stood there in front of 300 people in stage make-up, with memorized lines of three pages, with only the lights on me, and the skills necessary to fulfill that monologue are stupendous! Your memory must be sharp, your body must be alert, your heart must be strong, and your humility even stronger. Talk about fuel to the fire! Talk about a shot in the arm! This, is better than Botox.

Last week was International Woman's Day but I do invite all of us to keep celebrating womanhood everyday. I want us all to keep reminding women of choices that they can make; that they can choose anger and they can choose peace and they can choose silence and they can choose candor and they can choose to do battle and they can choose to watch and they can choose family and they can choose solitude and they can choose freedom and they can choose Life.

The ABCs of Family

A

A couple of nights ago, we trooped to the Cultural Center of the Philippines to watch Coke, my older brother, play with the Metro Manila Community Orchestra.

The whole family, especially my mother, was excited. He was going to play Bartok's Concerto # 2. Coke had informed us earlier that the piece was forty-one minutes of excruciating heaviness. The piece was composed on a 12-tone scale, which simply means it is not a melodious piece, nor a pleasant one. It was designed in order to illustrate musically the modern existence of mankind—an existence filled with alienation, despair, and extreme loneliness. He warned us that it would be difficult listening.

Crazily enough, this information did not deter me from bringing along two of my children. Watching concerts is part of our family identity. They've seen Tito Coke perform in many different kinds of theaters. They make nothing of the fact that this man who takes them to watch movies and heartily encourages their consumption of junk food is actually—gasp—a world-class performer.

It's difficult to describe what it feels like to watch a family member on stage. We are, essentially a family of performers, and it's a part of us I've always taken for granted. So much of our history is tied to this central gift—of translating experience into different art forms—for my brothers through music, for my sister and her husband through painting, and me through words.

In a way, this prescribed family identity made it easier to find myself as a person, while growing up. I see the children (mine and my sister's) watch us, and I get the feeling it might be easier for them as well because everyone is so sure of who they are in this family. Oh there will be difficulties, for certain, along the path. But half the battle has been won, because the battle is a worn path.

Watching Coke weave his magic, effortlessly convincing his audience to go on this modern journey, coaxing them to embrace their loneliness and desperation, I go through my own journey of remembering what it was like for him as an artist, having been privy to his struggles and his heartaches. I know what had to happen in the past in order for him to play this way, and we are both grateful.

I enjoy and struggle with the piece as much as he does as he plays it. I know what it means to lengthen a musical line for the sheer pleasure of it. I know he is thinking of our father in certain passages. I know he knows he has reached the artistic zone where his own creativity fuses with the creative spirit of the world. Maybe this is what drives performers to share to a public rather than just remain in their private spheres—the need to showcase a higher spirit that permeates the world.

B

Marty, my daughter, has started her own life of performing, even if she is only six. Before the end of the school year, she would have danced four times already. She is scheduled to perform in Miriam Ballet's yearly production. This year, they are staging "Peter Pan" at the AFP Theater.

As a parent, I had the option to let her join the recital or not. I stumbled on the decision for a while and wondered if I should, only because my family does not take performing lightly. But she said she was ready and I guess I had to be too.

She has rehearsals almost everyday and I never have to take care of her. She prepares her own things, keeps track of her own schedule and simply weaves in and out of this world like she was born into it. Once in a while, her hair is not as combed as it should be; or her shoes are not clean, as I know her Teacher Liza would want them to be. The lecture sits on my tongue and I always decide to let it go, only so that she may learn to fight her own battles.

Once I asked her what it was she wanted to be. She said she was certain she would not continue with the violin. She wants to continue with her dancing. I tease her that she will be the first Bolipata dancer. She wants to apprentice some more with her Tito and Tita because she wants to be a visual artist too. How wonderful that my children can take these options without wondering where to go for guidance.

A few months ago, she performed for the first time in school in front of a large, paying audience. If it is cathartic to watch a sibling on stage, it is disconcerting to watch your child on stage. There is pride certainly, as what it is asked of the child to do on stage is stupendous. There is fear as well, that she will not be strong enough to handle the job. There is nostalgia as I go back to my own life as a performer. And there is always that sense of rightness when I see her on stage—as if I know instinctively that it is her birthright and her destiny.

C

Marty sat to my left in the upper box, while my son, Teodoro sat with his father in the orchestra. I enjoy taking my kids on such cultural outings. I've taken them with me to other concerts, art openings, museum exhibits, etc. Our family schedule is filled with such events. For them, it is both culture and family. Yes, we will sit through this rehearsal, performance, exhibit, or whatever, for as long as it takes because then we will have dinner together and we will not go to school the next day! That's the way our mother raised us. She took us to all kinds of performances as well and each event would be punctuated by a humongous meal at Aristocrat near Malate. It never mattered what we might miss in school. It's hard to say now what was more educational—time with art, or time with family.

I watched my son from the upper box. My son does this move where he extends his arms and his legs when he listens to music. The doctors call it "spasmic." Some therapists have called it "inappropriate behavior." Strangers who've seen him do this must probably think it's "weird." We in the family call it "cute." It is a signal to us that he is in the zone of happiness. He does this the whole time Coke plays. It is the way music makes him feel. It courses through his underdeveloped body and wraps it in pleasure. The intensity of the music is made even more intense by the fact that it is his Tito Coke playing. At the end of the piece, he screams "Bravo!" unabashedly. My son is only 8 and yet I am convinced he knows music, the way I can never know it.

In our family, Teodoro is never seen as a problem to be solved. There are no discussions of doctors I should see, or people I should ask for help. Although family members get tired of his tiresome questions, nobody ever refuses to answer them. Tito Coke is willing to teach him violin again. Plet and Emong, my sister and her husband who are painters, help him with art activities. They're very good at calming him down. My sister Non helps him increase his musical knowledge by exposing him to the Beatles and to Joni Mitchell. Her kids are patient and loving when they play with him. Tito Chin, the older brother, has offered to help him with sports to improve his muscle tone and when he is bigger, to try the cello. My brother Jed, the pianist who lives in New York, sends me photographs of interesting places and faces for Teodoro's collection. Teodoro is in charge of walking my mother from her office to the terrace every day for lunch, a simple act that is capable of teaching my wild boy manners and responsibility. We've chosen to accept the language he knows and to use that language to teach him about this very square world. The family teaches him, not only because I asked them to, but also because they want to. This tribal, ancient activity of raising my unusual boy is a way for us to own him; to say to the world, "he is one of us."

We all see ourselves in Teodoro, sometimes painfully. Once, he had a terrible tantrum during family dinner. In the aftermath, we all sat together, breathless and quiet. No one offered a solution but instead, one by one, started to share their own examples of tantrums in their childhood, including my mother. Teodoro listened intently, his eyes moving from one family member to the next. It was wonderful for me then, to know that the intensity of this child is not a frightening thing— but rather, that it has history, and therefore, can have meaning. How wonderful for Teodoro to have learned that he is not at all strange, but rather at home, with family.

True or False

One of the most fun games I've ever played with a group is this game called Two Truths, One False. It's not a very good title (much too obvious and doesn't really sound right!) for a game, considering games should be fun, but, it is what it is, and all you have to do when your turn comes is to give two truths and one false thing about yourself. The people in the group will have to guess which is the lie.

Here are mine:

1. In 1986, during the People Power Revolution (I was sixteen), my best friend Lisa and I were at Camp Crame in the teeming crowd. We had finally gone, together with my father who was busy buying cigarettes for the soldiers, and my mother, who in true typical fashion, stayed in the car while it was parked along Santolan. We were in school early that day but they eventually sent us home. As soon as we were fetched (we were often at each other's homes) we went straight to the *palengke* and bought supplies. Lisa and I spent the afternoon cooking *munggo* and *pancit* to bring to the soldiers.

Due to the jostling in the crowd, we lost my dad but I had been trained well on what to do when lost. My parents were paranoid about such things. I knew that all I needed to do was stay in the exact same spot until he would find us. The idea that we could possibly be in any kind of danger seemed impossible at sixteen.

We had managed to remain fairly near the front, so we could see the arrival of newly-defected famous personalities from politics and show business. What happened next was almost unreal.

Freddie Aguilar came on stage where many showbiz personalities were singing and performing to buoy up the audience to keep them from going home. We were in the first row so I could hear the people in charge making decisions as to which singer would be next or what number would be next.

After a while, I could hear Freddie saying he needed someone to deliver a message to the forces stationed at Camp Aguinaldo. No one wanted to go and leave the safe haven at Camp Crame. In spite of the palpable sense of victory in the air, they knew they could still be arrested, killed, or picked up by enemy forces. Freddie sat on his haunches and searched the crowd. Freddie, as you know, has beautiful, piercing eyes. Much like a visionary his eyes roamed the crowd looking for a possible messenger. He sat there, completely calm and contained, certain that someone would be up to the task.

Something about the moment made me want to step up to the plate. Without Lisa knowing it, I had raised both our hands as volunteers. Freddie looked at me and must have asked himself if we were trustworthy. I told him that we were in our school uniforms as if that very fact proved our good intentions. He made us write down our names and phone numbers on a piece of paper. He handed me a letter, told me to look for Mr. _____ along the gate of the camp. He asked us to do our best to make sure that the message was safely in his hands.

But here's the funny part, more than being afraid of holding that message in my hands, crossing a great distance to the Camp, the possibility that I would fail in my mission and history would never be the same again, I was more afraid of leaving my spot and of never being found by my father again.

2. When I was in Grade 5, our teacher told us that visitors would come to our classroom to look for singers. These visitors she said were from a big recording company and were looking for new talent. Each classroom would then hold a competition and choose a representative to compete with other reps from other classes. In our class that simply meant either me, or another classmate named Gloria.

This was when I was young and so therefore completely fearless. The contest took three rounds. In the first round I sang "Where is Love" from the musical *Oliver*. This was always my competition piece and I sang it well because the song is perfect for my range. In the second round I sang "Somewhere Over the Rainbow" from the movie The Wizard of Oz. This was, and is, a difficult song to sing so I gave it my all.

In the final round, only Gloria and I remained, just as the class had predicted. Like me, Gloria was a fierce competitor. What added to the fearlessness of the moment was that she was one of my best friends. We were alike in many ways: we both came from artistic families; we were both misfits at school; we were both soaring sopranos. Something about her being my opponent made it more like a game. Often, at the end of class, we would wait for our *sundo* singing songs to each other! Losing to her, would not have been a problem.

For the final round I sang "People" from the movie *The Funny Girl*. I think that's what spelled the difference. I don't think the judges were prepared to hear a ten year old sing such an old song. I eventually won the contest. I won a recording contract and recorded children's songs that came out on tapes. It took me a little less than a year to record around fifty children's songs. If you've ever been to a children's party, a tape of children's songs is sure to be playing. That could be me singing "Head, Shoulders, Knees and Toes."

3. In the early '80s my brothers often came home to perform at the Cultural Center of the Philippines in between their studies. These were always major family events and our ordinary lives would shut down to accommodate the coming of the brothers. My sisters and I would not go to school for weeks and instead attend the rehearsals. The highlight was not really skipping school, and neither was it listening to classical music. The real highlight was being able to eat at Aristocrat along Roxas Boulevard. Our family lived in Malate for a decade so being in the area, visiting our old haunts was always pleasurable.

A week before the concert, my mother would take us to Shoe Mart along another boulevard, this time Aurora, and buy us our concert clothes. This was indeed another highlight. Our brothers would perform in coat tails or the finest Barong Tagalog. We wanted to look just as chic after all.

But there was another highlight. At these concerts, Madame Imelda Marcos would always make sure to come. You could feel her electric presence as soon as she would enter the lobby of the CCP. Photographers would click away and her gown would catch the flash of camera and magnify the light that always seemed to surround her. She would sweep in with such drama and I lived for the moment when she would come to the family and kiss us all. It really felt as if some of her magic remained with me.

One night, she invited the family to have dinner at Malacañang. Oh we were excited beyond belief. We were in a convoy so we could see her limousine. The palace gates opened and did not stop our old van from entering. We got down, and was I ever so happy that the dress I had on was grown-up and mature! I remember walking down the hall where the portraits of all the Presidents were hanging. The chandeliers seemed huge and the opulence of it all took my breath away.

Suddenly, we were in an elevator. I was surprised that such an old building could have such a contraption. I didn't know what to expect but I knew my life would never be the same. The doors opened and the hall was dark. We could see lights darting to and fro but I wasn't sure what that was all about. My mother's hand lay in mine and we entered, unsure if we had come to the right place. My father, a few steps ahead of us, disappeared into the darkness of the room. We followed and as my eyes adjusted, I couldn't believe it but lo and behold, it was a disco.

At the center was a strobe light causing the darts of light we had seen from the elevator. Cabinet members and their wives were dancing to '60s or maybe '70s music. Strung on the ceiling were Valentine decorations of angels and hearts. And there in the middle danced the Queen.

So there they are. My two truths and one lie. It is certainly true that one learns much about a person by what one believes to be the truth and even in the rendering of the truth. But far more interesting, perhaps, are the lies we spin and keep.

Yes, Margarita,
There Is a Santa Claus

Dear Marty,

Do you know that I remember every single present you received from Santa Claus from the moment you were born? When you turned one, you received a soap dish. When you turned two, you received a musical instrument. When you turned three, you got a baby chair. At four, it was a Barbie doll, much to my consternation. At five, it was a stuffed toy. When you turned six, it was a bike. And last year, you received a rock star microphone!

I can still reconstruct all your faces (including those of your *kulit*, adorable brothers) at the wonderment of receiving Santa's presents! Through the years you've built this relationship with him. There were years when you wrote him personal letters and it truly broke my heart when at five you wrote him for a dog. Your doctor advised against it and it was the one year you gave Santa several options! I can even remember moments when I caught you wanting to be good to impress him. How many times have I invoked his name to keep you and your brothers obedient!

But what I am about to do is quite difficult and I need you to hold my hand when I do it. I hope what I am about to tell you my dearest will not break your heart. I hope that you will not be angry with me and that if you will be angry, you will give me a chance to explain. (But I have great faith in you and in us!) It's time you know something very important. I am telling you now because I think you're old enough and will be able to understand what I am about to tell you. Here is the secret I promised to tell you last week: *there is no Santa Claus.*

I can almost see your face right now and I know you're in a bit of a quandary. You're not really sure what I mean so I thought I'd write you to find a way to make things easier. I won't pretend and tell you I have all the answers but I will do my best to explain things as clearly as I can.

The first thing it means is that the presents you've gotten every year since you were born on midnight of December 24 are presents not really from Santa but more from me and your daddy. We always took great pains to make it seem like the present did not come from the house. The present was never under the tree. I always used a different wrapper. The present would magically appear as the clock struck midnight. It has been a game between us, quite frankly.

First off, let me add that Santa Claus at some point did exist and his name in history is Saint Nicolas. I know you love stories so allow me to tell you his. He was a man famous for his generosity and his love for children. He lived a long time ago in 3 BC (that's thousands and thousands of years ago!) and he was originally from a part of Greece that is now Turkey (you remember the pictures I showed you of Greece?). He lived a life that was full of giving (he was even a Bishop!) and the stories that have remained about him always have the element of a surprise gift that arrives just when it is needed.

Here's one famous story about him, which I actually found on the internet and maybe later we can read the site together to know more about him:

One story tells of a poor man with three daughters. In those days a young woman's father had to offer prospective husbands something of value—a dowry. The larger the dowry, the better the chance that a young woman would find a good husband. Without a dowry, a woman was unlikely to marry. This poor man's daughters, without dowries, were therefore destined to be sold into slavery. Mysteriously, on three different occasions, a bag of gold appeared in their home—providing the needed dowries. The bags of gold, tossed through an open window, are said to have landed in stockings or shoes left before the fire to dry. This led to the custom of children hanging stockings or putting out shoes, eagerly awaiting gifts from Saint Nicholas. Sometimes the story is told with gold balls instead of bags of gold. That is why three gold balls, sometimes represented as oranges, are one of the symbols for St. Nicholas.

When St. Nicolas died and was buried, a unique relic appeared— a liquid substance was formed named manna and so devotion to him to this day remains. For sure there is a reason why the birth of Christ, which is what we truly celebrate, has become also synonymous with the story of Santa Claus. For sure it has something to do with the awesome gifts both brought into the world. For sure it has something to do with the way giving should be defined and practiced in this day and age.

You might be wondering why was it necessary to keep it a secret all these years? Why the world's concerted effort to keep the truth away from you? The answer is really quite simple. You see, is true giving is a lot like keeping a secret. When one truly gives, one does not trumpet one's generosity. When you open a present from Santa, it does not matter if Santa knows you or does not know you. It only matters that he has given you something freely. And giving something freely is also what Christ has done for you.

It is kept a secret because a large part of faith is wonderment. What the secret does is it ties you ever so closely to the idea of mystery. The mystery of who Santa is and the mystery of how the present lands in your hands and the mystery of how Santa knows just what you want allows you to feel the wonder of love and the surprise that comes with being loved absolutely. (And this might be hard for you to understand now but I do want you to know that at the heart of belief, of believing anything, is mystery. For how mysterious the ability to see beyond what can be seen. How mysterious the innate knowledge that the world is so much larger than our minds and hearts could ever comprehend.)

Does this make any sense, my love? Just think of the joy you receive when you hide from me when I come home from the office. Why hide? What's the thrill of being found? There are no answers because the answers reside in the heart. You hide because you know you will be found. You scream with joy at being found because you are proven some sense, it's also an exercise in practicing believing in what one cannot see.

I am sure your next question will be: "Why tell me the truth now Mom?" And that perhaps is an even harder question.

A few weeks ago, you had your first Communion. There's a reason why that's done when you're seven or eight. It is the age when you are able to discern more complex things. You are taught in class that the host that you take is the body of Christ and what is asked of you to believe is quite stupendous. (You see what I mean by mystery?)

I read once in a book that a child becomes a grown-up when he or she becomes aware of "metaphor." A metaphor is when one thing is used to stand for another. Like when you say "there's a rollercoaster in my tummy!" because it's all ya-yay or achy. The rollercoaster stands for that feeling in your ya-yay tummy. The host that you take is really *just* bread, baked and wrapped and sold. But through Communion, it becomes *more* than just bread. It becomes something else. It literally becomes Jesus Christ. That is an act of metaphor making.

To tell you the truth now is to show you clearly the metaphor behind Santa Claus. His present simply stands for what giving truly is. You already know the feelings and the emotions behind such a phenomenon. Now you are old enough to understand the thinking behind it and it is my wish as your mother that your heart and mind come together and know with your complete being that you have the capacity to also be a giver.

Do you remember that every morning when we have breakfast we see a butterfly hovering close by? We always say to the butterfly "Good Morning, Pappy!" although we know that Pappy, your grandfather is dead. You know he is dead because you were there when we said goodbye. I know that you know death already.

To believe that the butterfly that accompanies us when we have our toast and eggs is Pappy is a supreme act of faith. When we enunciate the words "Good Morning, Pappy," we testify to the largeness of life and the gift of spirit that continues even after death. Indeed, we have learned to see beyond what the physical eye can see! When I tell you Pappy is no longer with us, you know what I mean. And when I say, Pappy is still with us you also know what I mean. Perhaps that is the second sign of becoming more grown-up: understanding that irony and certainty can exist in peace.

Margarita, when I say, Santa Claus does not exist, by now you know what I mean. And when I say, Margarita, Santa Claus does exist, your heart also knows what I mean. This is my prayer for you on your eighth Christmas: that I have taught and you have learned a difficult but worthy lesson about love and giving.

Love,

Mom

A Father's Day Imagining

She said   Once again, he has not had breakfast with his children. And once again, he did not see them before they went to bed. He must see the children an average of ... what, fourteen full waking hours a week? Doesn't he know how much his children miss him and need him in their lives?

He wakes up so early and begins to prowl the house. I can hear his large footsteps echo through the walls and floors. I don't know what I wish for more: for him to be quiet so that they won't wake up too early; or that he be noisy enough to wake them so that they may see him today.

Once in a while, the prowling wakens someone. It is delicious to watch the child discover her daddy by the foot of the bed. The first few seconds of discovery are most precious. Here lies this moment filled with possibility. But the possibility is always short-lived because the phone at some point will ring.

I watch this from faraway and I realize that it doesn't matter to our child that the phone rings. (In my mind I've already scolded him for the intrusion of the office into this precious moment.) Her father's arm is around her waist and he keeps her close even as he accommodates the call. She watches his mouth in amazement and I realize he has to do so little to have an impact. Just this solid presence is enough. Maybe this is something I will never understand. I work hard at having my children respect my presence. All he has to do is show up—just like a movie star.

I look at him and wonder what he truly thinks of me. He does not know how much I miss just being the two of us. I clip the thought out right away and censor these thoughts I am told I am not allowed to have. Yes, I am still in love with my husband. Other marriages around me have fallen and sputtered and died out but ours remains burning by the grace of ... who knows by what or whose grace? Maybe by the children's grace for surely I cannot help but be reminded of our love every time I look into their precious eyes. But I am afraid sometimes. Does he still see me apart from the children? Without the children, who would we be? Most of our waking years is spent as parents not as husbands or wives. Maybe that's why we celebrate Father's Day or Mother's Day and not Husband's Day or Wife's Day.

Who was it that designed human life this way? We spend the best years of our lives at work and completely miss the childhoods of our children. When we are finally free of the demands of life and it is time to retire, our children will have all grown and we will barely recognize them; nor will they recognize us. How many children wish they knew their father more? Perhaps life should be built some other way. It makes no sense I know but let me think it anyway.

He said I wake up at five in the morning and wait for the sun to rise. I try to be quiet and be still so as not to wake the rest of the household but waking up early is a habit I cannot seem to break. No one knows how much I love this hour. I flit from room to room and accomplish a variety of things. I am able to inspect which light bulbs need to be changed. I discover that the fire alarm needs a new battery. I tighten the faucet in the children's bathroom. I test all the doorknobs to make sure all things are safe. I feel useful this way. If mothers are all about kisses and hugs; fatherhood is all about nuts and bolts. You need both elements to make a family work.

The sun is finally out in full force but the children refuse to wake up. I sit at the edge of their beds and wait for them patiently. I am not sure what is more delicious—observing them in sleep, smooth cheeks on pillow, a bit of dried up drool present; or the slow opening of the eyes to the world and the smile that descends upon seeing me on their beds.

More often than not, it is the former that actually happens. I sit and wait and watch but they rarely get up. I imagine their bodies recharging like batteries. Their mother will have to contend with all that renewed energy. My phone suddenly rings. It is only a little past six and already the outside world has made its presence felt.

I answer the phone automatically and I know that my wife's eyebrow is raised, wherever she is. There are some differences between us that can never be bridged and I am past trying to build bridges between lands that cannot meet. I will always answer the phone if the office calls. She thinks this is a matter of choice. I think otherwise.

In my mind's eye, I look at my wife and wonder what she truly thinks of me. She doesn't know how hurtful she can sometimes be with her quick judgments and harsh words. She tells me I am not present enough as a father. I look around our home and the lovely things that lie here and wish to tell her that this is my presence—the capacity to make this possible. If I were physically present all the time, we would be living in a hut. Women do not know how we men balance our choices as well.

I am still in love with my wife. It is a precious thing that keeps itself alive in spite the number of things that could kill it so easily. She does not know how grateful I am for the children. I wish I could tell her every day how glad I am that she is present for the children. I wish she knew how terrible it would be if I was the one who stayed at home! With her they read books, do art projects, sing and dance. I don't tell her that there are times when I imagine just being alone with them. I would teach my boy how to fly a kite. I would teach my girl how to climb a tree. These things make her nervous so I only dream about them.

I sometimes wonder who designed human life this way. Who was it that decided that fathers must work far away while mothers kept hearth and home? And so the little lives of my children are lost to me. I do not know my daughter's best friend's name; nor do I know my little boy's bedtime story.

Let me say it for the all fathers in the world. The lack of this knowledge is not a sign of a lack of love or interest. It is the limitation of the mind and body and not the heart. More than anything, it is contrast that makes life worth living. This constant defining of "mother" and "father" allows love to flourish more in some mysterious, wonderful way. It is good that no one person can be everything to any one. It allows us fathers and mothers to fill the different spaces in our children's lives.

Love Is the Thing in Life

When I was often fetched late from school I would while away the time in the classroom just either reading or writing on the blackboard. (Who knew back then that it would be a rehearsal for the life I'm leading now?)

What was it I would write on the blackboard? Normally, I would make my own quotations. These were easy to write because they would only contain one or two lines and they seemed to capture quickly and succinctly what seemed to be "the truth" to me. I had a big, black diary that came from an uncle who worked at Insular Life, and after I had filled the blackboard with these original quotations, I would write them down on this diary. I wish I could remember some of those quotations and I am saddened by the fact that the diary no longer exists.

However, there is one quote that remains. It remains with me because later on, I would make the effort to make letter cutouts, form this very short quotation and tape it to my desktop. I had gotten into this activity because all my father's secretaries (he had three and why he had three is certainly a story worth telling someday) would pepper their desks with pictures, sweet sayings and then later cover it with plastic wrap. The emotion wrapped up in all that activity resonated in my extremely young soul and I wished to copy it. The quotation is this: "Love is the thing in life."

An interior life is precious and all this activity of writing things down, naming them, concretizing them in cutout form, pasting and taping and wrapping was certainly an act of identification. How awful then that when this was all done, my family took one look at this desk of mine and started to make fun of it.

I go back to this story in my mind's eye and I can no longer recall what I felt. From where I am, it doesn't feel like it was anger I felt. It feels more like incredulity—as if I couldn't believe that they didn't know that this was the secret to all of life.

We envy children because of their youth. But I think we envy them more because they live life with the knowledge of truth more intimately.

As I write this, I am in the province of Zambales with my ten year old boy. Two of my siblings live here now: Coke, who is founder and Artistic Director of Casa San Miguel; and Plet, the painter. We live on a mango farm and here sits Casa, the arts center, my sister's house and me, in my old mother's house.

Our days are predictable, and this is more or less the point of this exercise. Predictability is the key to a stress-free life with a special child. We wake up at 7 in the morning and have breakfast together. He swims from 8 to 10 while I read or write. He listens to music until lunchtime. We have lunch together with my sister and her husband. In the early afternoon, he is allowed to watch one video. At around 3 p.m., he swims again. At 4 we take a walk to the beach or, if he prefers, to swing in the garden while I do my yoga. We have dinner at 6:15 before the sun has even descended completely. We watch another video together and he sleeps at 8:30 while I continue to read and write. Proper reading and writing is easier to do without the summer heat bearing down on me.

This week, something new arrived. Mark, the son of one of the carpenters on the farm, came to visit his father.

He is the same age as my son and there is relief for all. His father was happy that he is the same age as my son so they can play together and he can go about his carpentry without having to worry about his son. My son's therapist was happy because someone else can absorb the stress of entertaining him. Mark was happy because he becomes part of the predictability of my son's life. My son was happy that he had someone he could be with who is not a grown-up.

The relief turns into a strategic nightmare however, when the idea of social class begins to come into play. We ponder the protocol of where Mark should eat. Should he eat with us or with the rest of the carpenters? And if he were to eat with us, would he be sitting at the table with us? He wants to watch TV with my son and he asks why he cannot have his own choice of channel and why he can only watch what my son wants to watch. My son's therapist is at a loss on how to respond to this query. At lunch, Mark doesn't like the food and I don't know how to respond. He takes food from our pantry and from across the room his father fidgets, uncomfortable. I pass him an easy smile and we both know in that smile that things will be okay because this friendship will not last. Now the two of them want to have a sleepover, and his father and I look at each other and wait for each other's signals on whether this is okay or not.

These thoughts and ideas are part of the grown-ups' lives. These are problems made by grown-ups because we have been raised a certain way and there is no need to make judgments about the way we are raised. In that famous song from the musical *South Pacific*, the lieutenant sings "you've got to be taught" certain things. And these social games we play are part and parcel of things "we were taught." What is most frightening is the silence that accompanies this game. We all evaluate and shift our preconceived notions of people to accommodate new situations that come to us.

But to these two ten year olds, this is not a problem. These questions have not yet touched their interior lives. Judgments based on educational background, accomplishment, family membership, or employment have no bearing on friendship. They look at the grown-ups and wonder what all the hemming and hawing is about. They don't know it yet, but they are silently also being taught about their boundaries.

But for now, the beauty of summer is all that matters. How lucky for them that the grown-ups have no choice but to settle things between themselves. They swim together and the highlight is to jump and submerge themselves at the same time and look at each other under the water. The sheer pleasure of the other is crystal clear. They know with every fiber of their being this is the secret to all of life: love is the thing in life—love for the summer, for the water, for the friendship, for life itself—the pursuit of it, the finding of it, and the doing of it. The world of grown-ups, and the world of fear, is not yet theirs.

Kaldereta, Leche Flan, and Aristotle

There are days when I just want to give it all up and become a cook. I deliberately use the word "cook" rather than "chef." Cook is to writer as chef is to author and I would much rather be called a writer than an Author. A writer, to me, is someone who writes, someone who is obsessed with putting words on paper. There is a crudity and a primitivism to this act—the feeling that the act is a matter of survival; that to not put words on paper would mean certain death.

I like to cook. To me, it is one of the most relaxing activities. When I come home from work, I sometimes would much rather make brownies than play with my children. I like the method in cooking. I cook as if it were a contest with myself. How many dishes or plates or pots and pans or cooking utensils will I have to wash at the end of this dish? I love it when I am able to remain spare but produce a flavorful dish. To remain spare means to have a system—*mise en place*—the chefs call it: everything in its place. I like collecting things (bowls from the cabinet for a marinade, small bowls for chopped up vegetables from another cabinet, wooden spoons and measuring spoons from a drawer) to set up my *mise en place*.

The ancient philosopher Aristotle once said that human beings have an instinct for harmony. Our souls naturally long for the rhythm that surrounds us, in spite of the presence of cacophony or disharmony. We are natural at creating method as a system for achieving harmony. That is why when human beings hold babies, we naturally rock on our heels back and forth. It is as if we know, that babies will respond to this ancient rhythm. And so when we walk, we naturally find a step that is measured in time. When we do menial labor, such as folding laundry or sorting things in closet, a closer observation of the way we work will reveal a system of harmony. It is as if we know that the world hums around us and we are called upon by the world to hum with it.

I guess this is what resonates in me when I cook, or when anyone cooks. The rhythmic slicing of onions, the musical pounding on garlic, the pleasure of the hiss when water hits hot oil, arouses something in me and appeals to my sense of order. My children love watching me cook. They do not understand it when I write. But they understand my cooking.

But more real than a need for rhythm is a need for sustenance. Unlike animals where sustenance is a matter of survival, sustenance for human beings can become elevated to a moment of celebration, ritual, community, and love. Yes we eat and yes we need to eat, but part and parcel of this act is a need for nourishment for the soul. We commence this nourishment by beginning meals with prayer, for example. I personally love ladling food onto plates. The first two minutes of any meal in the house is begun with their mother ladling food. It is an act of love surely because to do so would mean to set their needs first. To do so would mean knowledge of what food pleases them. To do so would mean a way of my saying, "I love you" and let that knowledge nourish you.

A few months ago, I went to Canada and ironically enough learned to cook *kaldereta* and *leche flan*! We lived with my husband's old officemates in lovely Vancouver. I am sure many of you have experienced living with Filipinos abroad and what has always puzzled me are the dishes our hosts always decide to serve their guests.

Logic tells us that because we are visitors to a foreign land, we expect to be fed food of the new place. And so we expect perhaps salmon or halibut or hamburgers or "real" pizza and steaks. And yet, again and again, when living with Filipinos abroad, a veritable array of Filipino dishes are laid out in buffet style, the way it is done in fiesta time or Christmas time: *adobo, pancit, tinola, binagoongan,* and Filipino fried chicken (you know, the simple salty, crunchy one?). We as visitors partake of this but often think silently how strange it is that we are fed this way. We think, "don't they know this is the food we have everyday?" What then could possibly account for this behavior?

For one, it is an obvious sign that hospitality is tied to food. We open our doors to our countrymen as we would at home and we feed them what we would have fed them at home. To feed them foreign food would mean that they would literally "not feel at home." Hospitality is an expression concretized and what better way to do it than with food. The legal alien understands the crazy need for rice for a meal to feel like a real meal.

It is also perhaps a way of showing (not showing off) what one has become abroad but also what one still is. It has a double meaning, in some way. Yes I can afford this much food and I'm certain you have seen refrigerators and cabinets of Filipinos abroad where items are always big and plentiful. BUT, and it's a big but, although I can afford, there is nothing more satisfying than simple pancit. And yes, I can afford steak and halibut, but give me *danggit* anytime!

And perhaps in a much deeper way, Filipino food is served because the one is nourished is not really just the visitors. I think that the presentation of these foods is a silent question and what the legal (or illegal as the case may be) immigrant needs to know is that his or her old ways make sense. He or she needs to know that this harmony they have taken with them is real and useful. To partake of the food is acquiescence to that identity. In a foreign land, the Filipino can disappear and to have someone partake of original food is a way to say, "Yes I understand these dishes and I understand all that comes with it: the magnitude and variety of food because this is how we do it back home." It is therefore a conversation between the immigrant who is trying to find meaning in a new land and the visitor who is certain of himself and does not need the certainty of food to provide identity. Filipino grocery stores are a great way of saying out loud that someone understands in this new land the importance of Knorr seasoning! In this grocery where strange things such as *tenga ng daga* and bagoong and chicken cubes can be bought, nothing is strange because this is home.

I asked my host if I could help her cook for dinner and it was truly a wonderful moment. I absorbed the harmony in the making of the dish and our cooking together was a sharing not just of recipes but also of identities. Let me share with you then these dishes I learned while abroad. For certainly, these dishes taught me much about my own self.

KALDERETA

1 kilo beef bulalo cut
¼ cup Original Knorr seasoning
3 packs Mama Sita Kaldereta Mix
½ kilo potatoes
½ kilo carrots
½ kilo bell pepper
½ cup milk

Marinade beef in Knorr seasoning for around 10 minutes. In a stock pan, fry beef in hot corn oil. When brown on all sides, pour Mama Sita Kaldereta Mix, following instructions on the packet. Boil beef till soft for around 2 hours making sure to add water when necessary. Add potatoes, carrots and peppers after. Once all vegetables are done, add the milk and stir gently. Serve with hot, white rice!

LECHE FLAN

13 eggs
1 can condensed milk
1 can evaporated milk
2 teaspoons vanilla

Sauce:

1 cup water

½ cup sugar

Boil and set aside.

Separate egg yolks and place in separate container. Gently fold in condensed milk and evaporated milk and vanilla. Stir gently. Pour mixture over a piece of cheesecloth or a kitchen towel to further refine mixture. Do not over mix as this will make your leche flan uneven.

In baking dish, place cooled sugar mixture. Add yolk mixture. Bake in 200 degree oven for 45 minutes. Enjoy!

On Being Bolipata

I am asked all the time: what is it like to come from your family? So here's a real answer:

Every weekend, either a Saturday or a Sunday, it doesn't matter really, we all come together, to have family lunch. These meals are planned way ahead of time. This is mostly because my mother loves planning seeing all her children. It is also because we have different gustatory requirements and all our happinesses (if such a word exists and if it does not, it should) are important to her.

Let me introduce us the way our parents would: there is Jed, the pianist; Chin, the cellist; Plet, the painter; Coke, the violinist; Non the lawyer and then me, Rica, the writer. I never knew how unusual this manner of introduction was until only recently when my husband pointed out that in his family, people were introduced only by names plus order of birth, and not by the choices they had made of what it is they do in life.

(This is old news now but I hope you will indulge me. There's a bit of a need to explain whom the Bolipata Brothers are primarily because only one brother actively performs these days and we are more known now as the family who put up Casa San Miguel, an arts center in Zambales founded by my brother Coke in 1994. But before all this, and really 1994 was about giving back, my brothers were premiere Filipino musicians who studied abroad and reaped a harvest of awards for the country. Together, they toured all over America and Europe before disbanding and pursuing their own personal careers. Many people wonder why two of my brothers gave up performing and

Jed explained it this way to me: "If you've been performing since you were ten, at some point it becomes tiring and you ache for other things, other pursuits or other creative endeavors." For Jed, it is filmmaking and writing that is at the core of his artistic expression. For Chino, it is playing cello only for himself and his family.)

Jed is not at this table as he lives in New York. Chin and Coke come to the table from their respective apartments. Plet comes all the way from Zambales with her husband, the painter Elmer Borlongan. Non and I live in our parents' compound and we come with our husbands and children. "Yes," my father would say if he were still alive, "there are no daughters-in-law at this table." Until the day he died, my father was matchmaking nurses at the hospital for his bachelor sons. How he must have wanted his name to continue and how ironic that it has in a way he never imagined. For three years now, it has only been my mother who reigns over these lunches. She sits at the head of a table full of artists as she has done all these years.

I'm sure most of you want to know: what was in the water that my mother drank that made us so?

For one, blame it on genetics. My mother's father was Ramon Corpus, first Filipino concert violinist and first Filipino to study music abroad at the London Guildhall. He graduated in America at the New England Conservatory of Music, the premiere conservatory of its time. I am suspicious though that the first gene that can be blamed was that of a great-great grandfather, Vicente Ferriols, from Valencia, Spain, a conservatory-trained flutist on the Spanish armada that came to our shores. Transfixed by a Filipina's beauty named Lucia del Fierro, he set his roots here. Vicente was the archivist on this ship too and that perhaps explains the storytelling talent everyone in our family has.

My mother believes that this one moment brought together many elements—the centrality of Zambales to our creative spirit and the centrality of love and the importance of true love. But there is still another gene that makes this story even more complicated. My grandfather married a Magsaysay and from that gene perhaps came discipline and commitment. But here's an even greater suspicion: how

85

completely possible it is that it is my father's genes that make us who we are. Although he was a businessman, he was at heart a poet and certainly his temperament was artistic, tempestuous, and difficult to predict. More proof perhaps was his ability to make things happen from nothing.

When my parents first married, their business was a publishing house. One of their publications was called *Philippines International*, a literary magazine and even then, a life in the arts could not sustain them. To augment their income, they also printed yearbooks and schoolbooks. As more and more children came (and this I can imagine because I am a parent now who attempts to live on my art), he must have realized that it would just not be enough. I came as last child when my siblings were already artists so I can no longer imagine what our earlier life was like. But my mother remembers: "you cannot imagine how wonderful it was for them to come home from lessons and be told that they were beyond their years." Jed, the oldest, lived in our hardiest years and he practiced the piano on a book placed on my mother's lap. It would take a long time before my parents could even afford Coke and Chin their own instruments. Part of this story I guess would be the context of the times. They would not have been able to study abroad without the help of Imelda Marcos.

You cannot talk about the Bolipata Brothers without ultimately talking about the Bolipata sisters. Ours was a symbiotic relationship. Every night when we would pray the Rosary, my mother punctuated prayer with this line: "Dear God, thank you for the talents of the boys and the goodness of the girls." It was both lesson and prophecy. For the first two decades of our family life, the instructions were simple. The brothers pursued their music and the girls aided them with their goodness. Concretely that meant that Plet went abroad primarily to play guardian to prodigy brothers. That meant waking up the brothers and balancing their checkbooks and feeding them dinner and getting them to their rehearsals and shouting "Bravo!" at concerts. That meant that when they were home from studies in Juilliard, our lives (Non's and mine) in Manila shut down to accommodate the string of rehearsals and concerts and performances. We skipped school to be their assistants and because we always slept so late due to rehearsals and concerts. Between us and amongst us as siblings, there were no hard feelings. If anything, it was a heady time and we grew up always knowing that we always had each other, no matter what. In terms of our own artistic pursuits however, that would come for the girls, much, much later. For Plet, it would mean becoming a painter in her 30s in spite having known of that desire since she was a child. For me, it made me a closet writer for years. But that's another novel.

When I was born, we moved to a house in Marikina where we had very few neighbors. You'll laugh now but we had a stable of horses, my parents bred champion dogs, and our garden was as large as a small park so our days were filled with horseback riding and playing with dogs aptly named Melody, Sonata, and Brahms. My father attached speakers from one end of the house to another so that when Schubert was played, he was played everywhere. Our basement was a library and a music center and our nights were spent performing. The brothers would play (and really to me it was play) their instruments and we girls would sing. On some nights we presented dramas originally written by my brothers and we would make tickets and posters, never mind that only Ma and Pa were our audience. On rainy days, my father would take out a long table and we would paint the rain away. We would tack our artworks on the long wall in the hallway. These were happy, happy times. If you were to ask me therefore, apart from genetics, what made us expressive, it would be this kind of upbringing: an upbringing that valued and upheld the practice of fine arts.

This is much clearer to me now with the new generation of Bolipatas. They are visual artists and musicians and dancers and it is amazing to me how organic their talent is. Perhaps backed by history, they are less fearful and more certain because they know that they can run to a family member for guidance and even for apprenticeship. Maybe it is nature. But then without support, without the necessary scaffolding for art to flourish (you should see my kids calendar of activities: it's filled with artistic events!), it may eventually be un-chosen. So maybe it's nurture too.

I was once asked if being a Bolipata has an impact on my writing. I think that when you grow up, you only know family as family. It was only when I met other families when I realized how different we are-but that's a truth about all families. The impact on my art is definitely an exposure to it from birth, much like my mother, whose musical language is extensive. Its impact is on my aesthetic sensibility and my measure of beauty or what makes something beautiful. Its impact is on an understanding of audience and of having a responsibility to that audience. It is also in my own estimation of myself as I study my own development. (I grew up with music of the highest order all my life. Surely that has an impact on how I have developed?) More than anything, as I sit with them, every Saturday or Sunday lunch, it doesn't matter really, as we celebrate each achievement at this table, I realize that as in all families, my family has given me a soft place on which to fall.

Between Us While We Are Apart

I guess it's safe to say this out loud now: I have lost a friend. To say it out loud is a great admittance—a real acceptance of loss. All these years that I've suspected this loss, suspicion lay in my heart. For it to lay there meant it was in the domain of feeling and therefore "unreliable." To say it out loud means that it has moved to my mind and there lies knowledge and consciousness. I can say now with both mind and heart: I have lost a friend.

There's not much out there to help me navigate this loss. We have rules for other losses. When we lose objects, for example, we are asked: "when and where did you lose it?" We either go back to the place, look calmly (or in panic depends on the weight of the loss) for the possibility of stupid misplacement; or we go to other places that keep lost items. When it cannot be found, the choice is simple, we replace the object. Sure, we are irritated by such losses and yet it is still easier to accept because we know that these, at the end of the day, are mere objects.

Far more structured is the loss brought about by death. As death is the clearest, most final loss, it also has the most defined rules. There is a body to dispose of. There is a wake to survive. There is food to be served. There are letters to be answered. There are things to be put away. We have been guided, by example, on what to do to survive death. In this too, we have very little choice: we bury our dead and swallow our grief.

I have a suspicion that we don't know what to do when we lose a friend because we presume it is not as serious a loss. We think to ourselves, well, just find another friend! I understand now that that's ridiculous and that we are naïve. To lose a friend is to lose an ally, to lose history, to lose companionship, to lose a faithful mirror; I daresay, to lose a part of oneself.

Three questions then: why do we need friends? how do we lose friends? and what can one do when one loses a friendship?

The first question is perhaps the easiest. We take it for granted that friendships are natural. We don't always see that friendships are prerequisites to learning love. As in love, friendship requires recognition—acquiescence that there is something about the other that you like. It can be as simple as liking the same music, or the same books. After the initial recognition, it is the sustenance that becomes the challenge. How do we remain friends in the midst of our differences? How can I accommodate you in my busy life? How much of you can I accept? How much of me must I hide? How happy can I be for you?

That negotiation is crucial to healthy development. He who has good friends will perhaps find it easier to manage marriage, as good marriages are patterned after good friendships. And because good friendships are not contractual or formally ritualized, the friendships that we keep, I argue, are also quite sacred.

There are many wonderful things about friendship. There's great conversation and exhilarating debates. Why are these conversations and debates so much more fun than those in marriage? Simply because there's less expectation. We can argue for hours but I don't have to live with you! The fact that there are endings to coffee, to dinner, to a movie, gives friendships a freedom that cannot be found in marriage. The space between us allows us time to value the other and to look forward to seeing each other.

Speaking of freedom, without the complication of love and sexual tension and chemistry, friendships with the opposite sex promise a level of authenticity that's so crucial as one gets older. With real friends, I can eat a soup, a salad, an entrée (or two), dessert and coffee, and not have to apologize. I can cry like a baby and not have to hide. I can be angry as hell and know it will not be taken against me. I can be weak and not pretend that I'll be okay. I can be who I am in no relation to you (unlike in marriage where everything about me is about you and so my unhappiness can be taken as caused by spouse). The distance between us is what sets friends apart and allows them to appreciate each other. This is versus what distance is in marriage where it can be a bad thing because it can become a measure of the estrangement between us.

For me, the most wonderful thing about having a friend, and being a friend, is the sense that I am an archivist in some way. A friend of mine has been given the gift to remember for me who I am and who I wanted to be. A couple of months ago, I bumped into my best friend from Grade 6. She said, "You finally published your book!" I stood there in awe that she remembered. I stood there in awe that I had forgotten. I felt so reassured of the path I had taken because someone had remembered what it was I wanted even if I myself had forgotten.

How many times have we said of a friend, "she's no longer the person I know." Because that's what good friends do—they take spirit pictures of us. If I were to lose my way, all I would have to do is call an old friend and ask, "Who am I again?"

Friendships end for a number of reasons. Sometimes it's as painful as betrayal; and sometimes it's as simple as just not having enough time to nurture the friendship. Even here, maybe Darwin has the answer to why some friendships must die: the survival of the fittest. Only the strongest of friendships will last. Perhaps some friendships do not last forever, with good reason.

In my case, it is silence that has caused the loss. Like the good friend that I am, I send missives, keep my friend updated on who I have become. I invite my friend to witness my life still. I wave a flag from my tiny island to prove that I am still alive. But there is no word from the other land where my friend now resides. I see myself flashing a red flag in earnest. But nothing and no one waves back.

What then to do to survive losing a friend? I guess there are the usual palliatives—coffee with newer friends? A good book as it rains outside my window? Solitude is a good companion—at least there is no one to disagree with. Children and husband are good archivists too. And then there's work and work and work.

And perhaps there is still another choice: to have faith in the strength of one's friendship; to believe that the other has not forgotten and perhaps is only waylaid. I can wait in anticipation and hope that this distance between us will make us better friends and if not then to believe that what has transpired between us has value on its own and that to have had that is gift enough. For after all, part of friendship is trust.

This is a prayer I learned when I was young. An old friend, now lost, taught it to me. She used to say, as parting, "May God be between us, while we are apart." I finally know what that finally means.

"Hope Is the Thing with Feathers"

Hope is the thing with feathers
That perches in the soul,
And sings the tune without the words,
And never stops at all.

— Emily Dickinson

Today, I bumped into hopelessness. I don't bump into him often. I apologize for calling it a "him." It comes naturally to me, somehow. I am a woman, and more often than not, hopeful. So in my imagination, hopelessness is not feminine.

When I think of the word "hopeless," I think of this other beautiful word despair. I think it's beautiful because it sounds the way it should feel like. The air at the end of the word seems incapable of flight because of the harshness of the consonants *d*, *s*, and *p*. This is what despair feels like—a yearning hampered.

What am I like when I am in despair? My body breaks down. I begin to get mysterious illnesses—an unexplained malaise of some sort. I am functional enough and I rely on the steady reliability of time to get me through but I feel as if I am poised to weep, and all I need is the innocent question from a stranger to get me going. It's ridiculous really. The pain dulls my senses and heightens it at the same time. It's safe to say, hopelessness doesn't become me.

The first time I had met hopelessness with a ferocity that almost knocked me out was at the doctor's office years ago when I brought my special son to a specialist. We had been requested to send documentation of his everyday life so that they could have a fuller picture of him. My husband and I spent many months doing this documentation. We combed through his many pictures. As he is firstborn, and first *apo*, there was a picture for almost every day of his life. I had taped conversations between us and went out of my way to include a tape of us singing "The First Noel" together as it was a song he had learned even before he had spoken.

Unable to help myself, I made it a creative project. More importantly, I made it as authentic as it could possibly be. I wanted the doctors to see his brilliance, his excellence, and his potential. I wanted them to see beyond the limitations that were so obvious. In a sense, I wanted them to hope with me. What could back-up my hope? Well, here in my arms were the albums, the videotapes, the stories I could tell. (Once, I brought him to an art gallery. He took a look at all the paintings, took my hand, pointed to one and said, "*Baduy 'yon.*" He was only three at the time.)

It was the same feeling I had falling in love with my husband, strangely enough. I was in love not just with who he was at the moment; but because of love, I could see beyond the present and anticipate what his soul was going to be. It was the way I saw my son as well. The future loomed before me, and hope sang its wordless song and carried me in its wings.

We brought with us these albums, videotapes of parties, of other singing sessions with me. He was only four at the time and it felt as if I could recall every single day of his life thus far. He was in a different room with other doctors and I could see him from a one-way window and I knew he was not doing well. He was in flight mode and angry at being asked to do tasks he could not do. He began to smear the walls with spit. I stood there whispering, hoping that he would flash them a true picture of himself; hoping I could will it into being. Later on, a doctor would ask him to disrobe so that she could check his physiology His eyes turned to me, and he said: "Mommy, no more."

A few weeks later, the doctors saw us to tell us their findings. That was when I felt my first brush with despair. Perhaps that is it's first element—incongruity. Their version of him was incongruous from my version of him. It was much like reading a novel. We all looked at the same information and saw two different stories. I sat there for more than an hour and in the first few minutes I could feel the talons of hopelessness tring to find root in me.

And yet, something stronger and surer and faster came and I found not just hope, but ultimately love. I did nod when the doctors spoke of their findings and recommendations, but now I think, only as a gesture. I chose to believe in the possibility of the future, in the promise of tomorrow, and in the power of transformative love. I chose to believe that life could surprise me and that we (the doctors and I) did not know everything. There was great freedom there. There, there, there … finally a location where I could set a home, where I could build a family, where my soul could perch. What evidence did I have to back-up my hope? Nothing really; nothing but love. Hope can only beat with absolute love.

It has been many years since then and every day has been a working out of hope to its fullest capacity. He is ten now and he has hardly moved where his development is concerned. Those pictures we took seem to have frozen him as well. I sit here writing wondering if I was indeed wrong and had read all the signs incorrectly. The talons of despair find me and I am about to think that there is no hope left for us and tomorrow is just a dream I made up. But then, would that mean, there is no love left in me as well? It is a difficult question and one that I must deny everyday. Yes, there is love, even more than I ever thought possible. But it is not an easy love, and that fact has changed everything about me. Although hope cannot promise a happy ending and hope cannot will something into being unless it is time, the exercise of hope is an exercise of love.

How do I tell you about this journey my heart has embarked upon? The gift of this child to me is tremendous. Because of his presence, every day I am privy to the irony of life in every conceivable way (what could be more painful than being a teacher unable to teach my own son?). The world is literally like a hologram to me—move it this way, and the image looks flat; move it another way, and the other dimensions come alive.

I was once asked to concretize what it feels like to be his mother, and I said, it feels as if a secret has been revealed intimately to me by the world. And like all secrets, it is delicious to know, but overwhelmingly difficult to keep to myself and painful to carry on my own. Emily Dickinson must have known the secret as well, and was moved to write to tell us about it. It is my turn now. What is this secret that I can share with you? It is this: "You don't know how strong hope truly is, until you have truly battled with despair."

On Being Rich

My daughter tells me that she is caught in some kind of power play. Everyone in her class is busy deciding who is the richest of them all.

She is in grade school and trying to find her way and so when she begins stories like these, I make a mental effort to withhold judgment and allow her own spirit to make sense of things. It is hard work for a mother to remain impartial, to resist the urge to tattle to her teacher.

She tells me that they were making a survey of who had the most cars, the most houses, the most airconditioning units and the most *"baon."* I deliberately do not ask her what she said about us, her family and about the things that we own and do not own. I listen and instead ask what brought about the conversation. She says it was because a classmate had shown the contents of her wallet and everyone had oohed and aahed that she had with her a thousand pesos. I ask her if she oohed and aahed along. Sheepishly, she said yes.

I understand what it is like to be enthralled by wealth. (Through the days, she will reveal that this classmate has a swimming pool, a helicopter and a home in the States. My daughter's eyes will get bigger with each new revelation.) It is not as if I am over the fascination with it myself. The past few weeks I have been in the company of some of the wealthiest women (interviewing them for various writing jobs mostly) and interestingly enough, my daughter's struggles with defining self in relation to material wealth is a struggle I am in, as well.

I enter these wealthy people's homes and the *probinsiyana* in me is both shocked and envious. How I do long for linen napkins in my guest bathroom. How I do long for the perfectly designed-to-look-haphazard bouquet of blooms on my dining table. The tables are spotless and the houses are serene, calm, and efficiently run. The creases and edges of this world are less visible and the smells and sights are truly a feast for the senses. What a contrast to my crazy bits-and-pieces-sort-of-life where things don't quite match and where there is sure to be a tear here and there.

Wealthy women are always wearing just the right thing. I sit most uncomfortable in my *ukay-ukay* clothes that for some strange reason are always missing a button or do not close well enough. My jewelry does not shine as much and truth be told, I never quite know how to carry myself in such scenarios. Wealth whispers its own set of rules and its rules are hidden somewhere between the three sets of spoons and forks I need to navigate. Never having been privy to them, I am at a loss.

I watch these women and wonder if their lives are any less complicated than mine because they do not worry about the future the way I do. I wonder if that is a false notion. Because I do have friendships with other wealthy women (and I do have wealthy relatives I hardly see ...) I know that behind the expensive saltshakers are real and complex women. But I am adamant about believing that there exists a difference between us as women. Perhaps they worry about how to make their lives meaningful so that their wealth becomes useful. Perhaps they worry about how to raise good children. How difficult it must be to raise children who do not have a concept of not affording anything.

My daughter comes home distraught. I am glad that we are close enough for her to want to share with me right away what is troubling her. She tells me that she lied to her best friend about her wealth. She had claimed that her room had seventeen shelves (I know ... what an item to compete for!).

"But Mommy, she lied too. First she said she had twelve shelves. When I said I have seventeen, she changed her answer to thirty-five!"

I asked her why she lied. She merely shrugged. Of course, she does not really know, but I do. I know she lies because she thinks acceptance is tied to wealth. I know she lied because she is not yet strong enough to stand on her own. It takes courage to accept the limits of one's Self. How is she to say with pride, that in truth, she only has three shelves? How I wish I could figure this all out for her. We hugged and I told her that no matter what, she must know that she has her family to run home to and that there is no need for secrets in our home.

We are walking in the mall and our different versions of psychoses haunt us. I look at scented candles and want to duplicate a wealthy friend's house, which had so many candles you would literally not need to turn on any lights in her home. I am looking at plates and wondering if I have earned the right and the money to buy a new set of plates. She is looking at clips and girly accessories and the items she points out to are items I have seen on her classmates. Maybe we are fascinated with wealth because we presume that it is inextricably linked to freedom. How difficult it truly is to grow up! We both make concessions. I buy just one scented candle. I buy her a pair of clips. This is enough for us today. After all, we are holding hands.

While walking, she asks me if we are wealthy. I pause and this is what I say in my head. She might not be old enough to understand the truth of what I am about to say; but she is never too young to be told the complicated truth. I ask her how she would define wealthy or rich. She stares at me probably because it is a value she has merely inferred based on behavior. I tell her that there are different kinds of wealth. I say there's wealth that's tied to how much money one has in the bank. It could be about the number of friends one has. It could be about the ability to have a job or profession and the kind of work one is able to produce. It could be about talents and gifts one has. I tell her that material wealth is only about how much one has but that wealth is about many other things and that deep down we are all wealthy and rich in our own way.

This is a life-lesson for both of us, right here in the mall, in the middle of consumerism. As she studies her world, she is being taught that the ability to consume or to buy is what gives her value in society (a small one for now). I have to show her otherwise. I have to show her that value, lies within. To do that, I need to understand that this candle in my hand is nothing more than just a candle.

I need to pause here and tell you that there's one important thing I've learned in my years of teaching: children know when they are being lied to. They have that one gift that becomes dull in people as they grow up: the ability to tell a fake. It's a difficult lesson to learn but one that I always use on students and especially my children. They know when I am not straight with them and when I am not, I end up unraveling more than I bargained for.

I wasn't sure if I was able to get the message across. I wasn't sure if I had assuaged her fears. I wasn't sure if I helped to make her stronger. But this much I can tell you.

"Mommy," she tells me a week later, "I am nervous. I wrote her a letter of apology about my lie. I told her that I wasn't really rich, but that I am rich in talents and family."

The Lessons of Summer

Dedicated to Honey Carandang

I write this from my little balcony here on a mango farm in Zan
I've been calling home all summer. I can't believe summer is
over. You can tell by the way the air feels these days. You can e
by what's being sold at the mall. Gone are the summer dis
wading pools and swimming gear. Black school shoes, noteb
school bags have now replaced them. And of course althou
this is a perfect marketing ploy, I am grateful for the visu
that time moves on. Any day now, Christmas décor will b

But until then, until June rolls by, until I have to ab
my syllabus for the school year, my heart is still in Sum

I have been planting the past few weeks, improv
garden in front of my mother's old rickety house by
here during the summers with my children (in differen
sometimes two of them, or one of them or all of
them) and just am …

A few years ago, a good friend, much older a
told me that she realized sometime in her 40s: th
able to survive Manila life (or her life in genera
soul intact unless she could repair to a place, '
crowd." And so I've decided to do the same
style of course), renovating this old house pie
to do magic on my spirit. Memories flood n
house. It was built when my mother and I v
and she was 54) and back then I had no ir

built this house for her own need to repair. There is p
small unfolding in my understanding of my mother.

There are adventures for the picking here. Just last
typhoon Cosme rained all over us and I happened to be here b
with only my five-year old boy for company. At the edge of the
the sea so for three straight nights I could hear the relentless te
of waves and I did wonder what I would do if a tidal wave wa
occur. Absurdly, I do not know how to swim but the little boy do
Signal number 3 would eventually be declared and there was no powe
for two whole days. The house suffered some damage. What was most
amazing was that I discovered that the most fragile of flowers—the
santan, bougainvillea, rosal, etc. had managed to hold on. And yet, the
trees were not as lucky or as sturdy. But I'm getting ahead of myself,
trying to understand this particular summer's lessons.

When we were little, we spent all our summers here. My mother
loved these trips and she prepared them the way a general prepares
for war. I understand now how detailed she had to be to come up
here. Back then, all I did was get into the car. As a mother, I need to
think of every minute detail, which includes every tiny little thing.

Twenty years ago, many of my mother's aunts and cousins were
ll alive and this little town of San Antonio was filled with her own
ildhood memories. I loved coming home here, to listen to stories of
aunts and grandmothers about even more ancient people who
med large and mythical. I loved helping to string flowers for the
es de Mayo. I loved the reliability of market day where the town
sformed itself into one giant tiangge. And of course, there were all
e days by the sea—walking, swimming, boating, riding a carabao,
ting shells, picnicking by the shore, listening to cassette tapes of
Taylor and Basil Valdez while perched on a window ledge (of
e, attempting to look cool and angst-filled!), watching the slowest
sets, reading until the kerosene lamp could no longer be of any
erhaps this is the first real sign of ageing and I have become like
ndmothers—the nostalgia that has come upon me for days gone

Nostalgia brings with it the false sense of simplicity—the belief that the age gone before us was not only better but simpler. I know in my heart this is not true. I listened well to the stories of those ancient women and I know that they struggled with disease, war, and famine. Maybe the perceived simplicity was in the firm belief that all would be well: in the unflagging optimism over the goodness of man and of all things. They had won the battle over hopelessness in the face of adversity. And now, in old age, their stories seemed to say, "We have been proven right! See how beautifully we have survived!"

There are days when my children do not want to come here. As you know, I am not one to judge children and their feelings so as is my habit, I asked my daughter why. "I don't know, Mom. I don't know why." After much prodding, this is eventually what she said, "It's just not very comfortable here." Imagine the energy it took to curb my tongue! You see this is a lesson that is hard to learn in urban Manila: how to live with wildlife and the seeming endlessness of time. In Manila, there is little space for interesting creatures to grow. There are no fireflies, dragonflies, praying mantes, or grasshoppers. There aren't even any beds of *makahiya* anymore. Even ordinary things like the *gamu-gamo*, lizards that are slightly bigger, the infamous *tuko* (of which there are two noisy ones outside the bathroom here) are found only in books. There are also no *salagubang* or *salaginto* and how fascinated they were when they were taught how to tie up one with a piece of thread! By an old dead tree, a family of egrets had set a home and just recently, a shrike bird (which looks like a maya with a mask) was caught by hand! How strange it must be to them to have to share everything here with ants so large, you can actually see the parts of their body. This is after all not a resort so we cannot pretend to be fabulous. This is not a vacation (I can almost hear them say). This is our mother trying to teach us another "character-building" lesson!

And time yawns before them. The town is a good ten minutes away, by car, which we do not have when we are here. The most hip thing there is the Mister Donut stand that doesn't even have reliable store hours. Subic is a good forty-five minutes away. There is no television, no mall, nothing really but good old time (and preapproved DVDS!). But I sit quietly as they whine and complain, calling upon lessons I learned in my own childhood, trusting in nature's own teaching style, preferring for the change to come slowly and unobtrusively upon their young hearts and souls. There is so much to do with all this time. They swim. They read. We turn on music and they pretend to be rock stars. They play with sand and build forts. They paint. They watch men pick mangoes. They discovered the *sineguelas* and *santol* tree so they've learned to reserve "after swim time" going crazy over these fruits. (They recently learned how to open up the santol on their own!) They tear up and down the garden pretending to be Avatars. They draw. They snack relentlessly. They learn to accept boredom every day, which I am convinced is an important part of maturity. Who was it who taught us that all experiences should be entertaining?

And best of all are the little conversations that have the chance to be enunciated because of the collapsing of time. Frogs come out at night here and the noise terrifies the little boy more than anything else. His older sister says to him one night: "It's time to face your fears. If not now, when?" The other night, my daughter remembered her dead grandfather and she could not understand why she was happy and sad at the same time. I taught her a new word for such a feeling— bittersweet. The tuko calls in the middle of the night and they finally smile, finding his voice funny, their list of fears dwindling. Wisdom is absolutely priceless.

These past few nights, they have been obsessed with collecting salagubang. The little boy now knows how to allow the emerald-like creature to perch on his finger or his back. He knows that he has to wash his hands when it poops on him. Even more charming has been their knowledge that they must set free their collections of bugs at the end of the day. He kisses them on their backs, she strokes them and says comforting words about being together in an imagined future, they both pretend to shed a tear, and then they say goodbye. Once again, this is bittersweet. They do not know that they have learned a most important lesson.

And what about me? What have I learned? In the urban life, we expect to be gratified instantly. The accessibility of things muddles our sense not only of time but also of patience. I cannot stand having to wait for Yahoo! to load when actually if one were to really count, that waiting was not more than ten seconds. But ten seconds feels like something I cannot afford. I brought along this attitude when I first came here. I wanted the garden done in a week. I wanted the walls painted in a day. I wanted to be relaxed ALREADY. I wanted, wanted, wanted, now, now, now. But I am grateful to have relearned time. I am grateful that it has become a friend to me. I am grateful for its slowness. I am grateful for the reliable quiet of the first thirty minutes of each day. It is sublime, being able to watch bees pollinate the flowers by my window. I am grateful for time's own patience for people like me. The past few days, there is nothing more satisfying than taking my time.

In a few weeks, we will close this house and see it again next summer. We now plunge back into our normal, regular lives. Enrollment and the renewal of horrendously expensive car school stickers loom large in our futures. The real challenge is living these lessons even when geography alters. As I write this, a rare salaginto lands on the table. It is a precious, *precious* thing. His back glistens and catches the brightness of summer's light. I close my fingers over it. I will use him to wake the children.

From Whom All Good Things Come

Once, called upon to sit at the table of the fabulous Gilda Cordero Fernando (when the Queen of all Queens summons, one does not dare to not come), as we spread our artichoke dip on our Sky Flakes, I was casually asked about religion. I mentioned that although my siblings and I were raised Catholic, we were not all practicing Catholics. To which the equally fabulous guest to the right of Gilda sighed and said, "Ahhh, but that is because you have not yet lost your mother."

It was perhaps because the artichoke dip was so sinfully delicious (shred some canned artichokes, add four cloves of garlic minced well, 1 cup mayonnaise, 1 cup parmesan or mozzarella cheese, place into small ramekins, sprinkle some Spanish paprika on top and bake for forty minutes; yes, I called her afterwards to get the recipe), that no one pursued the point. Or maybe, like all prophecies, once uttered, it rendered everyone mute and dumb.

But it is an interesting nugget of an idea to mull over and think about, is it not? Why should the death of one's mother lead one to religion; and why not one's father but rather one's mother? Wouldn't any death of any one close to a human being lead the hardest of hearts to a recognition of a much higher power? And why in heaven's name did he have to utter it so capriciously, so truthfully, so matter-of-factly?

This last Christmas holiday we almost lost our mother. Of course today I say this out loud just as casually but there was a real fear there. She had a mild stroke and we were camped out at St. Luke's for a week. I think my heart kind of suspended itself as its own form of protection. I would go through the days filled with purpose and achieve them with precision but it felt as if nothing could touch me deeply. I did the usual gestures of hospital routine—you know, learning to manipulate the hospital bed, becoming used to the regular rhythm of being constantly wakened to watch my mother poked and probed. I knew the deal of washing utensils, opening that big tray of food, peeling oranges, placing the Nurse emergency button close to her, living on fast food to get through the day. I would wake up like clockwork and pack the same things over and over again and I wondered holding yet again the same novel that I packed on the first day why I held on to the belief that this would be a productive time for me to "catch up" on my reading. I was a fool. This was a time to simply love my mother.

I would remain like this—suspended—until someone would utter that terrible "how are you?" line and I would notice myself tear. Once, at the end of my shift at the hospital, I actually had a facial (how absurd is that?) and the pricking on my skin was almost like piercing that protective wall and I cried straight for a good eight hours. I could allow myself this and use the facial as my excuse but I cried even more at how perfect all these symbols were—the writer in me finding connections in all things. In my heart of hearts I cried at the possibility that Death had finally come to our doorstep and I was unprepared. Literally, my safety bubble had been pricked.

I guess we believe that mothers are indestructible. To many of us mortals, our mothers are the next best things to super heroes. Mothers do everything and can defy the regular laws of the world. I hold my mother responsible for all of my first loves—reading and writing (ok fine, even the dastardly wrong him). Reflecting on the way I view my mother and father, I realize how unfair I was. It did not disappoint me to learn that my father was human. It was almost as if I had expected it and strangely enough felt comfort in his frailty. But from my mother, I expected her to be much, much more. How that came to be I have no idea. I only know now that it has colored everything about our relationship and I feel a weight lifting at the cognizance of my misconception. And I feel such utter gratefulness that I had learned it finally, at a time when I can still mend broken fences.

She lives with me now, while she recovers and everyday I am moved by this turn of events. My siblings and I joke all the time that my mother and I are both Roosters in Chinese astrology and so can never live together. But I do not mind sharing my roost and making her rule my life, for now. Every day is like a gift that she is here and although there is stress and tension, there is also much laughter. At the end of bathing her, my children apply lotion on her legs, giggling the whole time. We play dominoes and Uno cards and she laughs when her grandchildren win. I sit with her at breakfast as she prays her rosary. I turn on her DVD and watch her girlish delight at watching Gidon Kremer play the violin. I peruse the different books on my shelves and wonder which one she might enjoy. At mealtimes, she conspiratorially asks me what her prize is for dessert. I allow her four sips of my coffee. It is our delicious secret.

Something is happening here—as she regains her strength, I regain mine as well, both as mother and daughter. To live in a multi-generational home is to have a chance to live with the past, the present and the future, all at the same time. My son asks me how old Lola is and we count the numbers to reach 75. He counts his own age, which is 5 and his eyes grow wide. He counts to 95 the age of his great grandmother and his eyes are even wider. He is at a loss making sense of all that Math and the impact the knowledge has on his life and yet he understands now why in subtraction it's called *difference*.

I look at my children, my mother and myself, we who span the centuries. I take a look at the issues I hold in my hands and realize that they are merely creations of my fear. My mother survived, and so will I. My mother is human, and so am I. It is hard to explain but the presence of my mother in the home provides a trajectory of what is essential to a good life—to a definition of what one must pursue because it is worth pursuing. The five-year old got it right when he said„ "Mom, families are for loving each other and isn't it awesome!" It is a clearer insight he has learned watching us all accommodate the presence of the grandmother in our home. And yes, I have found religion and it's even greater gift of faith. I sit in prayer and recall that line that defines God as someone "from whom all good things come." I understand this even more now, with my grown-up Self.

Why I Write

Because there are days when I understand Jude Law's nanny. After all, there he was, in all his yumminess. And there she was, in all her ... nanny-ness ... in what real world would make him notice her? Perhaps it was that moment when his son asked for a glass of juice and right as she closed the refrigerator door, there he was about to tack a reminder that she was in charge of picking up the kids that afternoon. Her hand on the door, his hand on the door, and Boom! life alters.

Perhaps life had disappointed her, had made her think there was more than the daily drudgery of breath to breath. How many children can one love? Maybe in this disappointment, and Jude offered his hand, she thought to herself, prayed to a being, "at least, let me have this." I am convinced she was thinking only of herself in this moment. I am convinced, as we grow older, that we hunger for life-altering moments more and more. At least, that's the way I would write it in a story.

And there are days when I understand Sylvia Plath more than I can understand myself. I know that moment in the day when life is so completely overwhelming that the only other option left is annihilation. Love for children is complete for Sylvia as it is for me, thus the decision to erase oneself instead of another. And there are days when I say this out loud and people get upset and I write this information down in my diary as a tally sheet and wonder about the numbers on the page.

And I wonder about Pluto and how he really feels to have been believed to be a planet and then to be demoted to something less. I think of all the tests I took in Science 5 and how I had to memorize all the planets and their features and wonder what to do with all this information, and while we're at it, with any information. If things are true, until proven otherwise, and since many things can be proven otherwise, eventually, well why even teach children that some things are constant? Do we not set them up for disappointment? In my writerly mind, the title of this story will be Pluto's Child and I will name this child Daisy and she will rediscover Pluto.

And there are moments when I travel and I realize that I use the word "beautiful" incessantly. People from another country to me always belong in some kind of painting and I can spend many minutes trying to unravel my thinking. Are these foreigners truly beautiful or it is merely my need to romanticize and idealize all things? But truly, why does light look so different in other lands? What about being in another place makes one aware of the curve of light? And what color is this light? Oh the winding routes my mind can take exploring this issue!

I wonder why we are kinder to strangers than we are to the people we hold most dear. Why am I more generous with others than with my own self? Why do things really happen in threes? When I conjure stories in my head, my characters inevitably go through three things: do I reinforce this pattern in the world through the word?

And there is the wealth of snapshots running in my head, oftentimes looking random but I know by now that my memory keeps them for material. Like sitting by the stairs waiting for tears to come when our dog died when I was twelve. It is not the memory of the dog I retain, it is that feeling of wanting to be consumed by grief and feeling strange that all I could feel was relief. That moment when I was sixteen and I heard our neighbor screaming at her child, thinking to myself I will never scream at my child. I wonder at the irony of that now after having screamed so much at my children since then. Or that moment of revelation when my brother drew my assignment for me when I was around five and I was touched by his talent (at five!). Or how weird it was that at least two teachers asked me to ask my brother to have something drawn for their visual aids. What word would describe that first moment when a child knows the grown-up is doing something wrong?

My days are consumed by the one need to name moment to moment—enfleshing the world into words so that they may be turned in my hand, in my palm, and what it is that sits in my heart, can sit in my hand instead, and be thrown away into the sea; or kept in my pocket as keepsake. I walk the seashore of life and decide which rocks to keep, which to discard, which to put away so that I may mix and match at some later date; call upon a memory to authenticate a point; call upon a look that rested on me to explain character motivation; always, always keeping score.

Moment to moment I think to myself, there must be a word for this obliterating kind of joy. There must be a word for this travesty, or this tragedy, or this grief. What is the word at the center of my grief? This word is both identification and spell. If I can say the word, and only say the word, I shall be healed.

People wonder what it is a writer does and it is difficult to explain as it is a job that requires treading the line between real and imagined. Another writer-friend, when newly married, complained once that everyone in the house she lived in with her husband would constantly ask her to do errands after all, "she wasn't doing anything." People want us to produce pages to prove that we have written. In writing, production and product are severely different things. I am asked often, "were you able to write?" And in my head I think, well … I was able to think, which is the lifeblood of all writing.

So, to many most of the time we really look like we're doing nothing because part of writing is the hocus pocus part. For me, that requires hours of staring and sitting. It is ephemeral, the work of catching and matching words with experience. I need to keep still to do this. And sometimes, the opposite is true: I need to keep moving for the experience to catch me this time. There are those sought for moments when it just magically happens, when crystallization occurs. But when one writes long enough, one knows that the Muse also paces her gifts so they cannot always be relied upon.

I know the signs when I know I have hit upon something. There comes an incessant need to nest, i.e., to decorate, beautify, or simply move furniture. I get weepy and for some strange reason, a British accent takes over and I mull over words and my tongue lolls around them like candy. I drive around Manila uttering sentences I've written, pondering on cadence and rhythm, the musician in me descending. My husband says I have this faraway look and cannot be reached. And eventually that voice comes to me and propels me to write. It commands me to document.

As I write this, a man with three sons sits across from me. We have gone beyond looking at each other as a man or a woman. Instantly, my mind records. We pass a look to each other, finding ourselves complicit in the rearing of children, in the difficulty of it, in the constant guessing that we do when we raise sons to become men and raise girls to become women, knowing ultimately that it is ourselves that we raise. It is a look that is both sad and triumphant. I file it away, knowing I will need that look in some later page.

The Author

Rica Bolipata-Santos earned her AB in Humanities and her Master's degree in English Literature from the Ateneo de Manila University in Quezon City, where she teaches. She is currently working on her PhD in Creative Writing at the University of the Philipines in Diliman, Quezon City. She has published popular articles in local magazines and newspapers and scholarly studies in academic journals.

In 2006, her essay "Ten Scenes" won 2nd place in the *Philippines Free Press* Literary Awards. Her first book *Love, Desire, Children, Etc.: Reflections of a Young Wife* (Milflores 2005) won the prestigious Madrigal-Gonzalez Best First Book Award in 2007.

The author is married to Dino Santos, with whom she has three children: Teodoro, Margarita, and Antonio. She is the youngest child of the artistic Bolipata family.